THE

NECESSARY ANGEL

THE
NECESSARY ANGEL

Essays on Reality and the Imagination

B Y

WALLACE STEVENS

VINTAGE BOOKS
A Division of Random House
New York

. . . I am the necessary angel of earth,

Since, in my sight, you see the earth again.

THE AURORAS OF AUTUMN

INTRODUCTION

ONE FUNCTION of the poet at any time is to discover by his own thought and feeling what seems to him to be poetry at that time. Ordinarily he will disclose what he finds in his own poetry by way of the poetry itself. He exercises this function most often without being conscious of it, so that the disclosures in his poetry, while they define what seems to him to be poetry, are disclosures of poetry, not disclosures of definitions of poetry. The papers that have been collected here are intended to disclose definitions of poetry. In short, they are intended to be contributions to the theory of poetry and it is this and this alone that binds them together.

Obviously, they are not the carefully organized notes of systematic study. Except for the paper on one of Miss Moore's poems, they were written to be spoken and this affects their character. While all of them were published, after they had served the purposes for which they were written, I had no thought of making a book out of them. Several years ago, when this was suggested, I felt that their occasional and more or less informal character made it desirable at least to postpone coming to a decision. The theory of poetry, as a subject of study, was something with respect to which I had nothing but the most ardent ambitions. It seemed to me to be one of the great subjects of study. I do not mean one more *Ars Poetica* having to do, say, with the techniques of poetry and perhaps with its history. I mean poetry itself, the naked poem, the imagination manifesting itself in its domination of words. The few pages that follow are, now, alas! the only realization possible to me of those excited ambitions.

But to their extent they are a realization; and it is because that is true, that is to say, because they seem to me to communicate to the reader the portent of the subject, if nothing more, that they are presented here. Only recently I spoke of certain poetic acts as subtilizing experience and varying appearance: "The real is constantly being engulfed in the unreal. . . . [Poetry] is an illumination of a surface, the movement of a self in the rock." A force capable of bringing about fluctuations in reality in words free from mysticism is a force independent of one's desire to elevate it. It needs no elevation. It has only to be presented, as best one is able to present it. These are not pages of criticism nor of philosophy. Nor are they merely literary pages. They are pages that have to do with one of the enlargements of life. They are without pretence beyond my desire to add my own definition to poetry's many existing definitions.

WALLACE STEVENS

ACKNOWLEDGMENT

The Noble Rider and the Sound of Words *was read at Princeton, as one of a group of essays by several persons on* The Language of Poetry, *made possible by the interest and generosity of Mr. and Mrs. Henry Church, and was published by the* Princeton University Press *in* 1942. The Language of Poetry *was edited by Allen Tate. The* Figure of the Youth as Virile Poet *was read at the Entretiens de Pontigny, a conference held at Mount Holyoke College in* 1943. *The essay was published in* Sewanee Review *the following year.* Three Academic Pieces *was read at Harvard on the basis of the Morris Gray Fund. Later, in* 1947, *it was published by* Partisan Review *and also by* Cummington Press. About One of Marianne Moore's Poems *was published in* Quarterly Review of Literature *in* 1948 *in a number in honor of Miss Moore.* Effects of Analogy *was read as a Bergen lecture at Yale and was published a little later, in* 1948, *in the* Yale Review. Imagination as Value *was read at Columbia before the English Institute and was included in the volume of* English Institute Essays 1948 *published by the* Columbia University Press *in* 1949. The Relations between Poetry and Painting *was read in New York at the Museum of Modern Art in* 1951 *and was thereafter pub-*

lished by the Museum as a pamphlet. In The Relations between Poetry and Painting the quotation from Leo Stein's Appreciation is printed with permission of Crown Publishers (copyright 1947 by Leo Stein).

The author is happy to say thanks to all these and, in particular, to the magazines and presses for the assignments of copyrights which have made it possible to gather these essays together.

CONTENTS

I

The Noble Rider

and the Sound of Words

IN THE *Phaedrus*, Plato speaks of the soul in a figure. He says:

Let our figure be of a composite nature—a pair of winged horses and a charioteer. Now the winged horses and the charioteer of the gods are all of them noble, and of noble breed, while ours are mixed; and we have a charioteer who drives them in a pair, and one of them is noble and of noble origin, and the other is ignoble and of ignoble origin; and, as might be expected, there is a great deal of trouble in managing them. I will endeavor to explain to you in what way the mortal differs from the immortal creature. The soul or animate being has the care of the inanimate, and traverses the whole heaven in divers forms appearing;—when perfect and fully winged she soars upward, and is the ruler of the universe; while the imperfect soul loses her feathers, and drooping in her flight at last settles on the solid ground.

We recognize at once, in this figure, Plato's pure poetry; and at the same time we recognize what Coleridge called Plato's dear, gorgeous nonsense. The truth is that we have scarcely read the passage before we have identified ourselves with the charioteer, have, in fact, taken his place and, driving his winged horses, are traversing the whole heaven. Then suddenly we remember, it may be, that the soul no longer exists and we droop in our flight and at last settle on the solid ground. The figure becomes antiquated and rustic.

I

What really happens in this brief experience? Why does this figure, potent for so long, become merely the emblem of a mythology, the rustic memorial of a belief in the soul and in a distinction between good and evil? The answer to these questions is, I think, a simple one.

I said that suddenly we remember that the soul no longer exists and we droop in our flight. For that matter, neither charioteers nor chariots any longer exist. Consequently, the figure does not become unreal because we are troubled about the soul. Besides, unreal things have a reality of their own, in poetry as elsewhere. We do not hesitate, in poetry, to yield ourselves to the unreal, when it is possible to yield ourselves. The existence of the soul, of charioteers and chariots and of winged horses is immaterial. They did not exist for Plato, not even the charioteer and chariot; for certainly a charioteer driving his chariot across the whole heaven was for Plato precisely what he is for us. He was unreal for Plato as he is for us. Plato, however, could yield himself, was free to yield himself, to this gorgeous nonsense. We cannot yield ourselves. We are not free to yield ourselves.

Just as the difficulty is not a difficulty about unreal

things, since the imagination accepts them, and since the poetry of the passage is, for us, wholly the poetry of the unreal, so it is not an emotional difficulty. Something else than the imagination is moved by the statement that the horses of the gods are all of them noble, and of noble breed or origin. The statement is a moving statement and is intended to be so. It is insistent and its insistence moves us. Its insistence is the insistence of a speaker, in this case Socrates, who, for the moment, feels delight, even if a casual delight, in the nobility and noble breed. Those images of nobility instantly become nobility itself and determine the emotional level at which the next page or two are to be read. The figure does not lose its vitality because of any failure of feeling on Plato's part. He does not communicate nobility coldly. His horses are not marble horses, the reference to their breed saves them from being that. The fact that the horses are not marble horses helps, moreover, to save the charioteer from being, say, a creature of cloud. The result is that we recognize, even if we cannot realize, the feelings of the robust poet clearly and fluently noting the images in his mind and by means of his robustness, clearness and fluency communicating much more than the images themselves. Yet we do not quite yield. We cannot. We do not feel free.

In trying to find out what it is that stands between Plato's figure and ourselves, we have to accept the idea that, however legendary it appears to be, it has had its vicissitudes. The history of a figure of speech or the history of an idea, such as the idea of nobility, cannot be very different from the history of anything else. It is the episodes that are of interest, and here the episode is that of our diffidence. By us and ourselves, I mean you and me; and yet not you and me as individuals but as representatives of a state of mind. Adams in his work on Vico makes the remark that the true history of the human race is a history of its progressive mental states. It is a remark of interest in this relation. We may assume that in the history of Plato's figure there have been incessant changes of response; that these changes have been psychological changes, and that our own diffidence is simply one more state of mind due to such a change.

The specific question is partly as to the nature of the change and partly as to the cause of it. In nature, the change is as follows: The imagination loses vitality as it ceases to adhere to what is real. When it adheres to the unreal and intensifies what is unreal, while its first effect may be extraordinary, that effect is the maximum effect that it will ever have. In Plato's figure, his imagination does not adhere to what is real. On the contrary, having created something unreal, it adheres to it and intensifies its unreality. Its first effect, its effect at first reading, is its maximum effect, when the imagination, being moved, puts us in the place of the charioteer, before the reason checks us. The case is, then, that we concede that the figure is all imagination. At the same time, we say that it has not the slightest meaning for us, except for its nobility. As to that, while we are moved by it, we are moved as observers. We recognize it perfectly We do not realize it. We understand the feeling of it, the robust feeling, clearly and fluently communicated. Yet we understand it rather than participate in it.

As to the cause of the change, it is the loss of the figure's vitality. The reason why this particular figure has lost its vitality is that, in it, the imagination adheres to what is unreal. What happened, as we were traversing the whole heaven, is that the imagination lost its power to sustain us. It has the strength of reality or none at all.

2

What has just been said demonstrates that there are degrees of the imagination, as, for example, degrees of vitality and, therefore, of intensity. It is an implication that there are degrees of reality. The discourse about the two elements seems endless. For my own part, I intend merely to follow, in a very hasty way, the fortunes of the idea of nobility as a characteristic of the imagination, and even as its symbol or alter ego, through several of the episodes in its history, in order to determine, if possible, what its fate has been and what has determined its fate. This can be done only on the basis of the relation between the imagination and reality. What has been said in respect to the figure of the charioteer illustrates this.

I should like now to go on to other illustrations of the relation between the imagination and reality and particularly to illustrations that constitute episodes in the history of the idea of nobility. It would be agreeable to pass directly from the charioteer and his winged horses to Don

Quixote. It would be like a return from what Plato calls "the back of heaven" to one's own spot. Nevertheless, there is Verrocchio (as one among others) with his statue of Bartolommeo Colleoni, in Venice, standing in the way. I have not selected him as a Neo-Platonist to relate us back from a modern time to Plato's time, although he does in fact so relate us, just as through Leonardo, his pupil, he strengthens the relationship. I have selected him because there, on the edge of the world in which we live today, he established a form of such nobility that it has never ceased to magnify us in our own eyes. It is like the form of an invincible man, who has come, slowly and boldly, through every warlike opposition of the past and who moves in our midst without dropping the bridle of the powerful horse from his hand, without taking off his helmet and without relaxing the attitude of a warrior of noble origin. What man on whose side the horseman fought could ever be anything but fearless, anything but indomitable? One feels the passion of rhetoric begin to stir and even to grow furious; and one thinks that, after all, the noble style, in whatever it creates, merely perpetuates the noble style. In this statue, the apposition between the imagination and reality is too favorable to the imagination. Our difficulty is not primarily with any detail. It is primarily with the whole. The point is not so much to analyze the difficulty as to determine whether we share it, to find out whether it exists, whether we regard this specimen of the genius of Verrocchio and of the Renaissance as a bit of uncommon panache, no longer quite the appropriate thing outdoors, or whether we regard it, in the language of Dr. Richards, as something inexhaustible to meditation or, to speak for myself, as a thing of a nobility responsive to the most minute demand. It seems, nowadays, what it may very well not have seemed a few years ago, a little overpowering, a little magnificent.

Undoubtedly, Don Quixote could be Bartolommeo Colleoni in Spain. The tradition of Italy is the tradition of the imagination. The tradition of Spain is the tradition of reality. There is no apparent reason why the reverse should not be true. If this is a just observation, it indicates that the relation between the imagination and reality is a question, more or less, of precise equilibrium. Thus it is not a question of the difference between grotesque extremes. My purpose is not to contrast Colleoni with Don Quixote. It is to say that one passed into the other, that one became and was the other. The difference between them is that Verrocchio believed in one kind of nobility and Cervantes, if he believed in any, believed in another kind. With Verrocchio it was an affair of the noble style, whatever his prepossession respecting the nobility of man as a real animal may have been. With Cervantes, nobility was not a thing of the imagination. It was a part of reality, it was something that exists in life, something so true to us that it is in danger of ceasing to exist, if we isolate it, something in the mind of a precarious tenure. These may be words. Certainly, however, Cervantes sought to set right the balance between the imagination and reality. As we come closer to our own times in Don Quixote and as we are drawn together by the intelligence common to the two periods, we may derive so much satisfaction from the restoration of reality as to become wholly prejudiced against the imagination. This is to reach a conclusion prematurely, let alone that it may be to reach a conclusion in respect to something as to which no conclusion is possible or desirable.

There is in Washington, in Lafayette Square, which is the square on which the White House faces, a statue of Andrew Jackson, riding a horse with one of the most beautiful tails in the world. General Jackson is raising his hat in a gay gesture, saluting the ladies of his generation. One looks at this work of Clark Mills and thinks of the remark of Bertrand Russell that to acquire immunity to eloquence is of the utmost importance to the citizens of a democracy. We are bound to think that Colleoni, as a mercenary, was a much less formidable man than General Jackson, that he meant less to fewer people and that, if Verrocchio could have applied his prodigious poetry to Jackson, the whole American outlook today might be imperial. This work is a work of fancy. Dr. Richards cites Coleridge's theory of fancy as opposed to imagination. Fancy is an activity of the mind which puts things together of choice, *not* the will, as a principle of the mind's being, striving to realize itself in knowing itself. Fancy, then, is an exercise of selection from among objects already supplied by association, a selection made for purposes which are not then and therein being shaped but have been already fixed. We are concerned then with an object occupying a position as remarkable as any that can be found in the United States in which there is not the slightest trace of the imagination. Treating this work as typical, it is obvious that the American will as a principle of the mind's being is easily satisfied in its efforts to realize itself in knowing itself. The statue may be dismissed, not without speaking of it again as a thing that at least makes us conscious of ourselves as we were, if not as we are. To that extent, it helps us to know ourselves. It helps us to know ourselves as we were and that helps us to know ourselves as we are. The statue is neither of the imagination nor of reality. That it is a work of fancy precludes it from being a work of the imagination. A glance at it shows it to be unreal. The bearing of this is that there can be works, and this includes poems, in which neither the imagination nor reality is present.

The other day I was reading a note about an American artist who was said to have "turned his back on the aesthetic whims and theories of the day, and established headquarters in lower Manhattan." Accompanying this note was a reproduction of a painting called *Wooden Horses*. It is a painting of a merry-go-round, possibly of several of them. One of the horses seems to be prancing. The others are going lickety-split, each one struggling to get the bit in his teeth. The horse in the center of the picture, painted yellow, has two riders, one a man, dressed in a carnival costume, who is seated in the saddle, the other a blonde, who is seated well up the horse's neck. The man has his arms under the girl's arms. He holds himself stiffly in order to keep his cigar out of the girl's hair. Her feet are in a second and shorter set of stirrups. She has the legs of a hammer-thrower. It is clear that the couple are accustomed to wooden horses and like them. A little behind them is a younger girl riding alone. She has a strong body and streaming hair. She wears a short-sleeved, red waist, a white skirt and an emphatic bracelet of pink coral. She has her eyes on the man's arms. Still farther behind, there is another girl. One does not see much more of her than her head. Her lips are painted bright red. It seems that it would be better if someone were to hold her on her horse. We, here, are not interested in any aspect of this picture except that it is a picture of ribald and hilarious reality. It is a picture wholly favorable to what is real. It is not without imagination and it is far from being without aesthetic theory.

3

These illustrations of the relation between the imagination and reality are an outline on the basis of which to indicate a tendency. Their usefulness is this: that they help to make clear, what no one may ever have doubted, that just as in this or that work the degrees of the imagination and of reality may vary, so this variation may exist as between the works of one age and the works of another. What I have said up to this point amounts to this: that the idea of nobility exists in art today only in degenerate forms or in a much diminished state, if, in fact, it exists at all or otherwise than on sufferance; that this is due to failure in the relation between the imagination and reality. I should now like to add that this failure is due, in turn, to the pressure of reality.

A variation between the sound of words in one age and the sound of words in another age is an instance of the pressure of reality. Take the statement by Bateson that a language, considered semantically, evolves through a series of conflicts between the denotative and the connotative forces in words; between an asceticism tending to kill language by stripping words of all association and a hedonism tending to kill language by dissipating their sense in a multiplicity of associations. These conflicts are nothing more than changes in the relation between the imagination and reality. Bateson describes the seventeenth century in England as predominately a connotative period. The use of words in connotative senses was denounced by Locke and Hobbes, who desired a mathematical plainness; in short, perspicuous words. There followed in the eighteenth century an era of poetic diction. This was not the language of the age but a language of poetry peculiar to itself. In time, Wordsworth came to write the preface to the second edition of the *Lyrical Ballads* (1800), in which he said that the first volume had been published, "as an experiment, which, I hoped, might be of some use to ascertain how far, by fitting to metrical arrangement a selection of the real language of man in a state of vivid sensation, that sort of pleasure and that quantity of pleasure may be imparted, which a Poet may rationally endeavour to impart."

As the nineteenth century progressed, language once more became connotative. While there have been intermediate reactions, this tendency toward the connotative is the tendency today. The interest in semantics is evidence of this. In the case of some of our prose writers, as, for example, Joyce, the language, in quite different ways, is wholly connotative. When we say that Locke and Hobbes denounced the connotative use of words as an abuse, and when we speak of reactions and reforms, we are speaking, on the one hand, of a failure of the imagination to adhere to reality, and, on the other, of a use of language favorable to reality. The statement that the tendency toward the connotative is the tendency today is disputable. The general movement in the arts, that is to say, in painting and in music, has been the other way. It is hard to say that the tendency is toward the connotative in the use of words without also saying that the tendency is toward the imagination in other directions. The interest in the subconscious and in surrealism shows the tendency toward the imaginative. Boileau's remark that Descartes had cut poetry's throat is a remark that could have been made respecting a great many people during the last hundred years, and of no one more aptly than of Freud, who, as it happens, was familiar with it and repeats it in his *Future of an Illusion*. The object of that essay was to suggest a surrender to reality. His premise was that it is the unmistakable character of the present situation not that the promises of religion have become smaller but that they appear less credible to people. He notes the decline of religious belief and disagrees with the argument that man cannot in general do without the consolation of what he calls the religious illusion and that without it he would not endure the cruelty of reality. His conclusion is that man must venture at last into the hostile world and that this may be called education to reality. There is much more in that essay inimical to poetry and not least the observation in one of the final pages that "The voice of the intellect is a soft one, but it does not rest until it has gained a hearing." This, I fear, is intended to be the voice of the realist.

A tendency in language toward the connotative might very well parallel a tendency in other arts toward the denotative. We have just seen that that is in fact the situation. I suppose that the present always appears to be an illogical complication. The language of Joyce goes along with the dilapidations of Braque and Picasso and the music of the Austrians. To the extent that this painting and this music are the work of men who regard it as part of the science of painting and the science of music it is the work of realists. Actually its effect is that of the imagination, just as the effect of abstract painting is so often that of the imagination, although that may be different. Busoni said, in a letter to his wife, "I have made the painful discovery that nobody loves and feels music." Very likely, the reason there is a tendency in language toward the connotative today is that there are many who love it and feel it. It may be that Braque and Picasso love and feel painting and that Schönberg loves and feels music, although it seems that what they love and feel is something else.

A tendency toward the connotative, whether in language or elsewhere, cannot continue against the pressure of reality. If it is the pressure of reality that controls poetry, then the immediacy of various theories of poetry is not what it was. For instance, when Rostrevor Hamilton says, "The object of contemplation is the highly complex and unified content of consciousness, which comes into being through the developing subjective attitude of the percipient," he has in mind no such "content of consciousness" as every newspaper reader experiences today.

By way of further illustration, let me quote from Croce's Oxford lecture of 1933. He said: "If . . . poetry is intuition and expression, the fusion of sound and imagery, what is the material which takes on the form of sound and imagery? It is the whole man: the man who thinks and wills, and loves, and hates; who is strong and weak, sublime and pathetic, good and wicked; man in the exultation and agony of living; and together with the man, integral with him, it is all nature in its perpetual labour of evolution. . . . Poetry . . . is the triumph of contemplation. . . . Poetic genius chooses a strait path in which passion is calmed and calm is passionate."

Croce cannot have been thinking of a world in which all normal life is at least in suspense, or, if you like, under blockage He was thinking of normal human experience.

Quite apart from the abnormal aspect of everyday life today, there is the normal aspect of it. The spirit of negation has been so active, so confident and so intolerant that the commonplaces about the romantic provoke us to wonder if our salvation, if the way out, is not the romantic. All the great things have been denied and we live in an intricacy of new and local mythologies, political, economic, poetic, which are asserted with an ever-enlarging incoherence. This is accompanied by an absence of any authority except force, operative or imminent. What has been called the disparagement of reason is an instance of the absence of authority. We pick up the radio and find that comedians regard the public use of words of more than two syllables as funny. We read of the opening of the National Gallery at Washington and we are convinced, in the end, that the pictures are counterfeit, that museums are impositions and that Mr. Mellon was a monster. We turn to a recent translation of Kierkegaard and we find him saying: "A great deal has been said about poetry reconciling one with existence; rather it might be said that it arouses one against existence; for poetry is unjust to men . . . it has use only for the elect, but that is a poor sort of reconciliation. I will take the case of sickness. Aesthetics replies proudly and quite consistently, 'That cannot be employed, poetry must not become a hospital.' Aesthetics culminates . . . by regarding sickness in accordance with the principle enunciated by Friedrich Schlegel: 'Nur Gesundheit ist liebenswürdig.' (Health alone is lovable.)"

The enormous influence of education in giving every-one a little learning, and in giving large groups consider-ably more: something of history, something of philoso-phy, something of literature; the expansion of the middle class with its common preference for realistic satisfac-tions; the penetration of the masses of people by the ideas of liberal thinkers, even when that penetration is indirect, as by the reporting of the reasons why people oppose the ideas that they oppose,—these are normal aspects of ev-eryday life. The way we live and the way we work alike cast us out on reality. If fifty private houses were to be built in New York this year, it would be a phenomenon. We no longer live in homes but in housing projects and this is so whether the project is literally a project or a club, a dormitory, a camp or an apartment in River House. It is not only that there are more of us and that we are actually close together. We are close together in every way. We lie in bed and listen to a broadcast from Cairo, and so on. There is no distance. We are intimate with people we have never seen and, unhappily, they are intimate with us. Democritus plucked his eye out because he could not look at a woman without thinking of her as a woman. If he had read a few of our novels, he would have torn himself to pieces. Dr. Richards has noted "the wide-spread increase in the aptitude of the average mind for self-dissolving introspection, the generally heightened awareness of the goings-on of our own minds, *merely as goings-on*." This is nothing to the generally heightened awareness of the goings-on of other people's minds,

merely as goings-on. The way we work is a good deal
more difficult for the imagination than the highly civilized
revolution that is occurring in respect to work indicates.
It is, in the main, a revolution for more pay. We have
been assured, by every visitor, that the American busi-
nessman is absorbed in his business and there is nothing
to be gained by disputing it. As for the workers, it is
enough to say that the word has grown to be literary.
They have become, at their work, in the face of the ma-
chines, something approximating an abstraction, an en-
ergy. The time must be coming when, as they leave the
factories, they will be passed through an air-chamber or
a bar to revive them for riot and reading. I am sorry to
have to add that to one that thinks, as Dr. Richards
thinks, that poetry is the supreme use of language, some
of the foreign universities in relation to our own appear
to be, so far as the things of the imagination are con-
cerned, as Verrocchio is to the sculptor of the statue of
General Jackson.

These, nevertheless, are not the things that I had in
mind when I spoke of the pressure of reality. These con-
stitute the drift of incidents, to which we accustom our-
selves as to the weather. Materialism is an old story and
an indifferent one. Robert Wolseley said: "True genius
. . . will enter into the hardest and dryest thing, enrich
the most barren Soyl, and inform the meanest and most
uncomely matter . . the baser, the emptier, the ob-
scurer, the fouler, and the less susceptible of Ornament
the subject appears to be. the more is the Poet's Praise

. . . who, as Horace says of Homer, can fetch Light
out of Smoak, Roses out of Dunghills, and give a kind
of Life to the Inanimate . . ." (Preface to Rochester's
Valentinian, 1685, *English Association Essays and
Studies* 1939). By the pressure of reality, I mean the
pressure of an external event or events on the conscious-
ness to the exclusion of any power of contemplation. The
definition ought to be exact and, as it is, may be merely
pretentious. But when one is trying to think of a whole
generation and of a world at war, and trying at the same
time to see what is happening to the imagination, particu-
larly if one believes that that is what matters most, the
plainest statement of what is happening can easily appear
to be an affectation.

For more than ten years now, there has been an
extraordinary pressure of news—let us say, news incom-
parably more pretentious than any description of it, news,
at first, of the collapse of our system, or, call it, of life;
then of news of a new world, but of a new world so un-
certain that one did not know anything whatever of its
nature, and does not know now, and could not tell
whether it was to be all-English, all-German, all-Russian,
all-Japanese, or all-American, and cannot tell now; and
finally news of a war, which was a renewal of what, if it
was not the greatest war, became such by this continua-
tion. And for more than ten years, the consciousness of
the world has concentrated on events which have made
the ordinary movement of life seem to be the movement
of people in the intervals of a storm. The disclosures of

the impermanence of the past suggested, and suggest, an impermanence of the future. Little of what we have believed has been true. Only the prophecies are true. The present is an opportunity to repent. This is familiar enough. The war is only a part of a war-like whole. It is not possible to look backward and to see that the same thing was true in the past. It is a question of pressure, and pressure is incalculable and eludes the historian. The Napoleonic era is regarded as having had little or no effect on the poets and the novelists who lived in it. But Coleridge and Wordsworth and Sir Walter Scott and Jane Austen did not have to put up with Napoleon and Marx and Europe, Asia and Africa all at one time. It seems possible to say that they knew of the events of their day much as we know of the bombings in the interior of China and not at all as we know of the bombings of London, or, rather, as we should know of the bombings of Toronto or Montreal. Another part of the war-like whole to which we do not respond quite as we do to the news of war is the income tax. The blanks are specimens of mathematical prose. They titillate the instinct of self-preservation in a class in which that instinct has been forgotten. Virginia Woolf thought that the income tax, if it continued, would benefit poets by enlarging their vocabularies and I dare say that she was right.

If it is not possible to assert that the Napoleonic era was the end of one era in the history of the imagination and the beginning of another, one comes closer to the truth by making that assertion in respect to the French

Revolution. The defeat or triumph of Hitler are parts of a war-like whole but the fate of an individual is different from the fate of a society. Rightly or wrongly, we feel that the fate of a society is involved in the orderly disorders of the present time. We are confronting, therefore, a set of events, not only beyond our power to tranquillize them in the mind, beyond our power to reduce them and metamorphose them, but events that stir the emotions to violence, that engage us in what is direct and immediate and real, and events that involve the concepts and sanctions that are the order of our lives and may involve our very lives; and these events are occurring persistently with increasing omen, in what may be called our presence. These are the things that I had in mind when I spoke of the pressure of reality, a pressure great enough and prolonged enough to bring about the end of one era in the history of the imagination and, if so, then great enough to bring about the beginning of another. It is one of the peculiarities of the imagination that it is always at the end of an era. What happens is that it is always attaching itself to a new reality, and adhering to it. It is not that there is a new imagination but that there is a new reality. The pressure of reality may, of course, be less than the general pressure that I have described. It exists for individuals according to the circumstances of their lives or according to the characteristics of their minds. To sum it up, the pressure of reality is, I think, the determining factor in the artistic character of an era and, as well, the determining factor in the artistic character of an individual. The resistance to this pressure or its evasion in the case of individuals of extraordinary imagination cancels the pressure so far as those individuals are concerned.

4

Suppose we try, now, to construct the figure of a poet, a possible poet. He cannot be a charioteer traversing vacant space, however ethereal. He must have lived all of the last two thousand years, and longer, and he must have instructed himself, as best he could, as he went along. He will have thought that Virgil, Dante, Shakespeare, Milton placed themselves in remote lands and in remote ages; that their men and women were the dead —and not the dead lying in the earth, but the dead still living in their remote lands and in their remote ages, and living in the earth or under it, or in the heavens—and he will wonder at those huge imaginations, in which what is remote becomes near, and what is dead lives with an intensity beyond anv experience of life. He will consider that although he has himself witnessed, during the long period of his lite, a general transition to reality, his own measure as a poet, in spite of all the passions of all the lovers of the truth, is the measure of his power to abstract himself, and to withdraw with him into his abstraction the reality on which the lovers of truth insist. He must be able to abstract himself and also to abstract reality, which he does by placing it in his imagination. He knows perfectly that he cannot be too noble a rider, that he cannot rise up loftily in helmet and armor on a horse of imposing bronze. He will think again of Milton and of what was said about him: that "the necessity of writing for one's living blunts the appreciation of writing when it bears the mark of perfection. Its quality disconcerts our hasty writers; they are ready to condemn it as preciosity and affectation. And if to them the musical and creative powers of words convey little pleasure, how out of date and irrelevant they must find the . . . music of Milton's verse." Don Quixote will make it imperative for him to make a choice, to come to a decision regarding the imagination and reality; and he will find that it is not a choice of one over the other and not a decision that divides them, but something subtler, a recognition that here, too, as between these poles, the universal interdependence exists, and hence his choice and his decision must be that they are equal and inseparable. To take a single instance: When Horatio says,

Now cracks a noble heart. Good night, sweet prince,
And flights of angels sing thee to thy rest!

are not the imagination and reality equal and inseparable? Above all, he will not forget General Jackson or the picture of the *Wooden Horses*.

I said of the picture that it was a work in which everything was favorable to reality. I hope that the use of that bare word has been enough. But without regard to its range of meaning in thought, it includes all its natural images, and its connotations are without limit. Bergson describes the visual perception of a motionless object as the most stable of internal states. He says: "The object may remain the same, I may look at it from the same side, at the same angle, in the same light; nevertheless, the vision I now have of it differs from that which I have just had, even if only because the one is an instant later than the other. My memory is there, which conveys something of the past into the present."

Dr. Joad's comment on this is: "Similarly with external things. Every body, every quality of a body resolves itself into an enormous number of vibrations, movements, changes. What is it that vibrates, moves, is changed? There is no answer. Philosophy has long dismissed the notion of substance and modern physics has endorsed the dismissal. . . . How, then, does the world come to appear to us as a collection of solid, static objects extended in space? Because of the intellect, which presents us with a false view of it."

The poet has his own meaning for reality, and the painter has, and the musician has; and besides what it means to the intelligence and to the senses, it means something to everyone, so to speak. Notwithstanding this, the word in its general sense, which is the sense in which I have used it, adapts itself instantly. The subject-matter of poetry is not that "collection of solid, static objects extended in space" but the life that is lived in the scene that it composes; and so reality is not that external scene but the life that is lived in it. Reality is things as they are. The general sense of the word proliferates its special senses. It is a jungle in itself. As in the case of a jungle, everything that makes it up is pretty much of one color. First, then, there is the reality that is taken for granted, that is latent and, on the whole, ignored. It is the comfortable American state of life of the eighties, the nineties and the first ten years of the present century. Next, there is the reality that has ceased to be indifferent, the years when the Victorians had been disposed of and intellectual minorities and social minorities began to take their place and to convert our state of life to something that might not be final. This much more vital reality made the life that had preceded it look like a volume of Ackermann's colored plates or one of Töpfer's books of sketches in Switzerland. I am trying to give the feel of it. It was the reality of twenty or thirty years ago. I say that it was a vital reality. The phrase gives a false impression. It was vital in the sense of being tense, of being instinct with the fatal or with what might be the fatal. The minorities began to convince us that the Victorians had left nothing behind. The Russians followed the Victorians, and the Germans, in their way, followed the Russians. The British Empire, directly or indirectly, was what was left and as to that one could not be sure whether it was a shield or a target. Reality then became violent and so remains. This much ought to be said to make it a little clearer that in speaking of the pressure of reality, I am thinking of life in a state of violence, not physically violent, as yet, for us in America, but physically violent for millions of our friends and for still more millions of our enemies and spiritually violent, it may be said, for everyone alive.

A possible poet must be a poet capable of resisting or evading the pressure of the reality of this last degree, with the knowledge that the degree of today may become a deadlier degree tomorrow. There is, however, no point to dramatizing the future in advance of the fact. I confine myself to the outline of a possible poet, with only the slightest sketch of his background.

5

Here I am, well-advanced in my paper, with everything of interest that I started out to say remaining to be said. I am interested in the nature of poetry and I have stated its nature, from one of the many points of view from which it is possible to state it. It is an interdependence of the imagination and reality as equals. This is not a definition, since it is incomplete. But it states the nature of poetry. Then I am interested in the role of the poet and this is paramount. In this area of my subject I might be expected to speak of the social, that is to say sociological or political, obligation of the poet. He has none. That he must be contemporaneous is as old as Longinus and I dare say older. But that he *is* contemporaneous is almost inevitable. How contemporaneous in the direct sense in which being contemporaneous is intended were the four great poets of whom I spoke a moment ago? I do not think that a poet owes any more as a social obligation than he owes as a moral obligation, and if there is any-

thing concerning poetry about which people agree it is
that the role of the poet is not to be found in morals. I
cannot say what that wide agreement amounts to because
the agreement (in which I do not join) that the poet is
under a social obligation is equally wide. Reality is life
and life is society and the imagination and reality; that
is to say, the imagination and society are inseparable.
That is pre-eminently true in the case of the poetic drama.
The poetic drama needs a terrible genius before it is any-
thing more than a literary relic. Besides the theater has
forgotten that it could ever be terrible. It is not one of
the instruments of fate, decidedly. Yes: the all-command-
ing subject-matter of poetry is life, the never-ceasing
source. But it is not a social obligation. One does not
love and go back to one's ancient mother as a social obli-
gation. One goes back out of a suasion not to be denied.
Unquestionably if a social movement moved one deeply
enough, its moving poems would follow. No politician
can command the imagination, directing it to do this or
that. Stalin might grind his teeth the whole of a Russian
winter and yet all the poets in the Soviets might remain
silent the following spring. He might excite their imagi-
nations by something he said or did. He would not com-
mand them. He is singularly free from that "cult of
pomp," which is the comic side of the European disaster;
and that means as much as anything to us. The truth is
that the social obligation so closely urged is a phase of
the pressure of reality which a poet (in the absence of
dramatic poets) is bound to resist or evade today. Dante

in Purgatory and Paradise was still the voice of the Middle Ages but not through fulfilling any social obligation. Since that is the role most frequently urged, if that role is eliminated, and if a possible poet is left facing life without any categorical exactions upon him, what then? What is his function? Certainly it is not to lead people out of the confusion in which they find themselves. Nor is it, I think, to comfort them while they follow their readers to and fro. I think that his function is to make his imagination theirs and that he fulfills himself only as he sees his imagination become the light in the minds of others. His role, in short, is to help people to live their lives. Time and time again it has been said that he may not address himself to an élite. I think he may. There is not a poet whom we prize living today that does not address himself to an élite. The poet will continue to do this: to address himself to an élite even in a classless society, unless, perhaps, this exposes him to imprisonment or exile. In that event he is likely not to address himself to anyone at all. He may, like Shostakovich, content himself with pretence. He will, nevertheless, still be addressing himself to an élite, for all poets address themselves to someone and it is of the essence of that instinct, and it seems to amount to an instinct, that it should be to an elite, not to a drab but to a woman with the hair of a pythoness, not to a chamber of commerce but to a gallery of one's own, if there are enough of one's own to fill a gallery. And that élite, if it responds, not out of complaisance, but because the poet has quickened it, because he has educed from it that for which it was searching in itself and in the life around it and which it had not yet quite found, will thereafter do for the poet what he cannot do for himself, that is to say, receive his poetry.

I repeat that his role is to help people to live their lives. He has had immensely to do with giving life whatever savor it possesses. He has had to do with whatever the imagination and the senses have made of the world. He has, in fact, had to do with life except as the intellect has had to do with it and, as to that, no one is needed to tell us that poetry and philosophy are akin. I want to repeat for two reasons a number of observations made by Charles Mauron. The first reason is that these observations tell us what it is that a poet does to help people to live their lives and the second is that they prepare the way for a word concerning escapism. They are: that the artist transforms us into epicures; that he has to discover the possible work of art in the real world, then to extract it, when he does not himself compose it entirely; that he is *un amoureux perpétuel* of the world that he contemplates and thereby enriches; that art sets out to express the human soul; and finally that everything like a firm grasp of reality is eliminated from the aesthetic field. With these aphorisms in mind, how is it possible to condemn escapism? The poetic process is psychologically an escapist process. The chatter about escapism is, to my way of thinking, merely common cant. My own remarks about resisting or evading the pressure of reality mean escapism, if analyzed. Escapism has a pejorative sense, which it cannot be supposed that I include in the sense in which I use the word. The pejorative sense applies where the poet is not attached to reality, where the imagination does not adhere to reality, which, for my part, I regard as fundamental. If we go back to the collection of solid, static objects extended in space, which Dr. Joad posited, and if we say that the space is blank space, nowhere, without color, and that the objects, though solid, have no shadows and, though static, exert a mournful power, and, without elaborating this complete poverty, if suddenly we hear a different and familiar description of the place:

> *This City now doth, like a garment, wear*
> *The beauty of the morning, silent bare,*
> *Ships, towers, domes, theatres, and temples lie*
> *Open unto the fields, and to the sky;*
> *All bright and glittering in the smokeless air;*

if we have this experience, we know how poets help people to live their lives. This illustration must serve for all the rest. There is, in fact, a world of poetry indistinguishable from the world in which we live, or, I ought to say, no doubt, from the world in which we shall come to live, since what makes the poet the potent figure that he is, or was, or ought to be, is that he creates the world to which we turn incessantly and without knowing it and that he gives to life the supreme fictions without which we are unable to conceive of it.

And what about the sound of words? What about no-

bility, of which the fortunes were to be a kind of test of
the value of the poet? I do not know of anything that will
appear to have suffered more from the passage of time
than the music of poetry and that has suffered less. The
deepening need for words to express our thoughts and
feelings which, we are sure, are all the truth that we
shall ever experience, having no illusions, makes us listen
to words when we hear them, loving them and feeling
them, makes us search the sound of them, for a finality,
a perfection, an unalterable vibration, which it is only
within the power of the acutest poet to give them. Those
of us who may have been thinking of the path of poetry,
those who understand that words are thoughts and not
only our own thoughts but the thoughts of men and
women ignorant of what it is that they are thinking, must
be conscious of this: that, above everything else, poetry is
words; and that words, above everything else, are, in
poetry, sounds. This being so, my time and yours might
have been better spent if I had been less interested in
trying to give our possible poet an identity and less in-
terested in trying to appoint him to his place. But unless
I had done these things, it might have been thought that
I was rhetorical, when I was speaking in the simplest
way about things of such importance that nothing is
more so. A poet's words are of things that do not exist
without the words. Thus, the image of the charioteer and
of the winged horses, which has been held to be precious
for all of time that matters, was created by words of
things that never existed without the words. A descrip-

tion of Verrocchio's statue could be the integration of an illusion equal to the statue itself. Poetry is a revelation in words by means of the words. Croce was not speaking of poetry in particular when he said that language is perpetual creation. About nobility I cannot be sure that the decline, not to say the disappearance of nobility is anything more than a maladjustment between the imagination and reality. We have been a little insane about the truth. We have had an obsession. In its ultimate extension, the truth about which we have been insane will lead us to look beyond the truth to something in which the imagination will be the dominant complement. It is not only that the imagination adheres to reality, but, also, that reality adheres to the imagination and that the interdependence is essential. We may emerge from our *bassesse* and, if we do, how would it happen if not by the intervention of some fortune of the mind? And what would that fortune of the mind happen to be? It might be only commonsense but even that, a commonsense beyond the truth, would be a nobility of long descent.

The poet refuses to allow his task to be set for him. He denies that he has a task and considers that the organization of materia poetica is a contradiction in terms. Yet the imagination gives to everything that it touches a peculiarity, and it seems to me that the peculiarity of the imagination is nobility, of which there are many degrees. This inherent nobility is the natural source of another, which our extremely headstrong generation regards as false and decadent. I mean that nobility which is **our**

spiritual height and depth; and while I know how diffi-
cult it is to express it, nevertheless I am bound to give a
sense of it. Nothing could be more evasive and inacces-
sible. Nothing distorts itself and seeks disguise more
quickly. There is a shame of disclosing it and in its defi-
nite presentations a horror of it. But there it is. The fact
that it is there is what makes it possible to invite to the
reading and writing of poetry men of intelligence and de-
sire for life. I am not thinking of the ethical or the sono-
rous or at all of the manner of it. The manner of it is, in
fact, its difficulty, which each man must feel each day
differently, for himself. I am not thinking of the solemn,
the portentous or demoded. On the other hand, I am
evading a definition. If it is defined, it will be fixed and it
must not be fixed. As in the case of an external thing,
nobility resolves itself into an enormous number of vibra-
tions, movements, changes. To fix it is to put an end to
it. Let me show it to you unfixed.

Late last year Epstein exhibited some of his flower
paintings at the Leicester Galleries in London. A com-
mentator in *Apollo* said: "*How with this rage can beauty
hold a plea* . . . The quotation from Shakespeare's 65th
sonnet prefaces the catalogue. . . . It would be apropos
to any other flower paintings than Mr. Epstein's. His
make no pretence to fragility. They shout, explode all
over the picture space and generally oppose the rage of
the world with such a rage of form and colour as no
flower in nature or pigment has done since Van Gogh."

What ferocious beauty the line from Shakespeare puts

on when used under such circumstances! While it has its modulation of despair, it holds its plea and its plea is noble. There is no element more conspicuously absent from contemporary poetry than nobility. There is no element that poets have sought after, more curiously and more piously, certain of its obscure existence. Its voice is one of the inarticulate voices which it is their business to overhear and to record. The nobility of rhetoric is, of course, a lifeless nobility. Pareto's epigram that history is a cemetery of aristocracies easily becomes another: that poetry is a cemetery of nobilities. For the sensitive poet, conscious of negations, nothing is more difficult than the affirmations of nobility and yet there is nothing that he requires of himself more persistently, since in them and in their kind, alone, are to be found those sanctions that are the reasons for his being and for that occasional ecstasy, or ecstatic freedom of the mind, which is his special privilege.

It is hard to think of a thing more out of time than nobility. Looked at plainly it seems false and dead and ugly. To look at it at all makes us realize sharply that in our present, in the presence of our reality, the past looks false and is, therefore, dead and is, therefore, ugly; and we turn away from it as from something repulsive and particularly from the characteristic that it has a way of assuming: something that was noble in its day, grandeur that was, the rhetorical once. But as a wave is a force and not the water of which it is composed, which is never the same, so nobility is a force and not the manifestations of which it is composed, which are never the same. Possibly this description of it as a force will do more than anything else I can have said about it to reconcile you to it. It is not an artifice that the mind has added to human nature. The mind has added nothing to human nature. It is a violence from within that protects us from a violence without. It is the imagination pressing back against the pressure of reality. It seems, in the last analysis, to have something to do with our self-preservation; and that, no doubt, is why the expression of it, the sound of its words, helps us to live our lives.

II

The Figure of the Youth

as Virile Poet

I

I<small>T APPEARS</small> that what is central to philosophy is its least valuable part. Note the three scraps that follow. First, part of a letter from Henry Bradley to Robert Bridges, as follows:

My own attitude towards all philosophies old and new, is very sceptical. Not that I despise philosophy or philosophers; but I feel that the universe of being is too vast to be comprehended even by the greatest of the sons of Adam. We do get, I believe, glimpses of the real problems, perhaps even of the real solutions; but when we have formulated our questions, I fear we have always substituted illusory problems for the real ones.

This was in reply to a letter from Bridges, in which Bridges appears to have commented on Bergson. Then, second, it is Bergson that Paul Valéry called

peut-être l'un des derniers hommes qui auront exclusivement, profondément et supérieurement pensé, dans une époque du monde où le monde va pensant et méditant de moins en moins. . . . Bergson semble déjà appartenir à un âge révolu, et son nom est le dernier grand nom de l'histoire de l'intelligence européenne.

And yet, third, it is of Bergson's *L'Evolution Créatrice* that William James said in a letter to Bergson himself:

You may be amused at the comparison, but in finishing it I found the same after-taste remaining as after finishing Madame Bovary, *such a flavor of persistent* euphony.

2

If these expressions speak for any considerable number of people and, therefore, if any considerable number of people feel this way about the truth and about what may be called the official view of being (since philosophic truth may be said to be the official view), we cannot expect much in respect to poetry, assuming that we define poetry as an unofficial view of being. This is a much larger definition of poetry than it is usual to make. But just as the nature of the truth changes, perhaps for no more significant reason than that philosophers live and die, so the nature of poetry changes, perhaps for no more significant reason than that poets come and go. It is so easy to say in a universe of life and death that the reason itself lives and dies and, if so, that the imagination lives and dies no less.

Once on a packet on his way to Germany Coleridge was asked to join a party of Danes and drink with them. He says:

I went, and found some excellent wines and a dessert of grapes with a pine-apple. The Danes had christened me Doctor Teology, and dressed as I was all in black, with large shoes and black worsted stockings, I might certainly have passed very well for a Methodist missionary. However I disclaimed my title. What then may you be . . . Un philosophe, perhaps? It was at that time in my life in which of all possible names and characters I had the greatest disgust to that of un philosophe. . . . The Dane then informed me that all in the present party were Philosophers likewise. . . . We drank and talked and sung, till we talked and sung altogether; and then we rose and danced on the deck a set of dances.

As poetry goes, as the imagination goes, as the approach to truth, or, say, to being by way of the imagination goes, Coleridge is one of the great figures. Even so, just as William James found in Bergson a persistent euphony, so we find in Coleridge, dressed in black, with large shoes and black worsted stockings, dancing on the deck of a Hamburg packet, a man who may be said to have been defining poetry all his life in definitions that are valid enough but which no longer impress us primarily by their validity.

To define poetry as an unofficial view of being places it in contrast with philosophy and at the same time establishes the relationship between the two. In philosophy we attempt to approach truth through the reason. Obviously this is a statement of convenience. If we say that in poetry we attempt to approach truth through the imagination, this, too, is a statement of convenience. We must conceive of poetry as at least the equal of philosophy. If truth is the object of both and if any considerable number of people feel very sceptical of all philosophers, then, to be brief about it, a still more considerable number of people must feel very sceptical of all poets. Since we expect rational ideas to satisfy the reason and imaginative ideas to satisfy the imagination, it follows that if we are sceptical of rational ideas it is because they do not satisfy the reason and if we are sceptical of imaginative ideas it is because they do not satisfy the imagination. If a rational idea does not satisfy the imagination, it may, nevertheless, satisfy the reason. If an imaginative idea does not satisfy the reason, we regard the fact as in the nature of things. If an imaginative idea does not satisfy the imagination, our expectation of it is not fulfilled. On the other hand, and finally, if an imaginative idea satisfies the imagination, we are indifferent to the fact that it does not satisfy the reason, although we concede that it would be complete, as an idea, if, in addition to satisfying the imagination, it also satisfied the reason. From this analysis, we deduce that an idea that satisfies both the reason and the imagination, if it happened, for instance, to be an idea of God, would establish a divine beginning and end for us which, at the moment, the reason, singly, at best proposes and on which, at the moment, the imagination, singly, merely meditates. This is an illustration. It seems to be elementary, from this point of view, that the poet, in order to fulfill himself, must accomplish a poetry that satisfies both the reason and the imagination. It does not follow that in the long run the poet will find himself in the position in which the philosopher now finds himself. On the contrary, if the end of the philosopher is despair, the end of the poet is fulfillment, since the poet finds a sanction for life in poetry that satisfies the imagination. Thus, poetry, which we have been thinking of as at least the equal of philosophy, may be its superior. Yet the area of definition is almost an area of apologetics. The look of it may change a little if we consider not that the definition has not yet been found but that there is none.

3

Certainly the definition has not yet been found. You will not find it in such works as those on the art of poetry by Aristotle and Horace. In his edition of Aristotle's work Principal Fyfe says that Aristotle did not even appreciate poetry. In the time of Aristotle, there was no such word as literature in Greek. Yet today poetry is literature more often than not; for poetry partakes of what may be called the tendency to become literature. Life itself partakes of this tendency, which is a phase of the growth of sophistication. Sophistication, in turn, is a phase of the development of civilization. Aristotle understood poetry to be imitation particularly of action in drama. In Chapter 6, Aristotle states the parts of tragedy, among them thought and character, which are not to be confused. He says that character in a play is that which reveals the moral purpose of the agents, i.e., the sort of thing they seek or avoid—hence, there is no room for character in a speech on a purely indifferent subject. The annotation of the editor is this:

A man who chooses, e.g., vengeance rather than safety reveals his character by exercise of Will. A man who at dinner chooses grouse rather than rabbit reveals nothing, because no sane man would choose otherwise.

This sort of thing has nothing to do with poetry. With our sense of the imaginative today, we are bound to consider a language that did not contain a word for literature as extraordinary even though the language was the language of Plato. With us it is not a paradox to say that poetry and literature are close together. Although there is no definition of poetry, there are impressions, approximations. Shelley gives us an approximation when he gives us a definition in what he calls "a general sense." He speaks of poetry as created by "that imperial faculty whose throne is curtained within the invisible nature of man." He says that a poem is the very image of life expressed in its eternal truth. It is "indeed something divine. It is at once the centre and circumference of knowledge . . . the record of the best and happiest moments of the happiest and best minds . . . it arrests the vanishing apparitions which haunt the interlunations of life." In spite of the absence of a definition and in spite of the impressions and approximations we are never at a loss to recognize poetry. As a consequence it is easy for us to propose a center of poetry, a *vis* or *noeud vital*, to which, in the absence of a definition, all the variations of definition are peripheral. Sometimes we think that a psychology of poetry has found its way to the center. We say that poetry is metamorphosis and we come to see in a few lines descriptive of an eye, a hand, a stick, the essence of the matter, and we see it so definitely that we say that if the philosopher comes to nothing because he fails, the poet may come to nothing because he succeeds. The philosopher fails to discover. Suppose the poet discovered and had the power thereafter at will and by intelligence to reconstruct us by his transformations. He would also have the power to destroy us. If there was, or if we believed that there was, a center, it would be absurd to fear or to avoid its discovery.

Since we have no difficulty in recognizing poetry and since, at the same time, we say that it is not an attainable acme, not some breath from an altitude, not something that awaits discovery, after which it will not be subject to chance, we may be accounting for it if we say that it is a process of the personality of the poet. One does not have to be a cardinal to make the point. To say that it is a process of the personality of the poet does not mean that it involves the poet as subject. Aristotle said: "The poet should say very little *in propria persona*." Without stopping to discuss what might be discussed for so long, note that the principle so stated by Aristotle is cited in relation to the point that poetry is a process of the personality of the poet. This is the element, the force, that keeps poetry a living thing, the modernizing and ever-modern influence. The statement that the process does not involve the poet as subject, to the extent to which that is true, precludes direct egotism. On the other hand, without indirect egotism there can be no poetry. There can be no poetry without the personality of the poet, and that, quite simply, is why the definition of poetry has not been found and why, in short, there is none. In one of the really remarkable books of the day, *The Life of Forms in Art*, Henri Focillon says:

Human consciousness is in perpetual pursuit of a language and a style. To assume consciousness is at once to assume form. Even at levels far below the zone of definition and clarity, forms, measures and relationships exist. The chief characteristic of the mind is to be constantly describing itself.

This activity is indirect egotism. The mind of the poet describes itself as constantly in his poems as the mind of the sculptor describes itself in his forms, or as the mind of Cézanne described itself in his "psychological landscapes." We are talking about something a good deal more comprehensive than the temperament of the artist as that is usually spoken of. We are concerned with the whole personality and, in effect, we are saying that the poet who writes the heroic poem that will satisfy all there is of us and all of us in time to come, will accomplish it by the power of his reason, the force of his imagination and, in addition, the effortless and inescapable process of his own individuality.

It was of the temperament of the artist that Cézanne

spoke so frequently in his letters, and while we mean something more, so, it seems, did Cezanne. He said:

Primary force alone, id est *temperament, can bring a person to the end he must attain.*

Again:

With a small temperament one can be very much of a painter. It is sufficient to have a sense of art. . . . Therefore institutions, pensions, honours can only be made for cretins, rogues and rascals.

And again, this time to Emile Bernard:

Your letters are precious to me . . . because their arrival lifts me out of the monotony which is caused by the incessant . . . search for the sole and unique aim. . . . I am able to describe to you again . . . the realization of that part of nature which, coming into our line of vision, gives the picture. Now the theme to develop is that—whatever our temperament or power in the presence of nature may be—we must render the image of what we see.

And, finally, to his son:

Obviously one must succeed in feeling for oneself and in expressing oneself sufficiently.

4

An attempt has been made to equate poetry with philosophy, and to do this with an indication of the possibility that an advantage, in the long run, may lie with poetry; and yet it has been said that poetry is personal. If it is personal in a pejorative sense its value is slight and it is not the equal of philosophy. What we have under observation, however, is the creative process, the personality of the poet, his individuality, as an element in the creative process; and by process of the personality of the poet we mean, to select what may seem to be a curious particular, the incidence of the nervous sensitiveness of the poet in the act of creating the poem and, generally speaking, the physical and mental factors that condition him as an individual. If a man's nerves shrink from loud sounds, they are quite likely to shrink from strong colors and he will be found preferring a drizzle in Venice to a hard rain in Hartford. Everything is of a piece. If he composes music it will be music agreeable to his own nerves. Yet it is commonly thought that the artist is independent of his work. In his chapter on "Forms in the Realm of the Mind," M. Focillon speaks of a vocation of substances, or technical destiny, to which there is a corresponding vocation of minds; that is to say, a certain order of forms corresponds to a certain order of minds. These things imply an element of change. Thus a vocation recognizes its material by foresight, before experience. As an example of this, he refers to the first state of the *Prisons* of Piranesi as skeletal. But "twenty years later, Piranesi returned to these etchings, and on taking them up again, he poured into them shadow after shadow, until one might say that he excavated this astonishing darkness not from the brazen plates, but from the living rock of some subterranean world." The way a poet feels when he is writing, or after he has written, a poem that completely accomplishes his purpose is evidence of the personal nature of his activity. To describe it by exaggerating it, he shares the transformation, not to say apotheosis, accomplished by the poem. It must be this experience that makes him think of poetry as possibly a phase of metaphysics; and it must be this experience that teases him with that sense of the possibility of a remote, a mystical *vis* or *noeud vital* to which reference has already been made. In *The Two Sources of Morality and Religion*, Bergson speaks of the morality of aspiration. It implicitly contains, he says,

the feeling of progress. The emotion . . . is the enthusiasm of a forward movement. . . . But antecedent to this metaphysical theory . . . are the simpler representations . . . of the founders of religion, the mystics and the saints. . . . They begin by saying that what they experience is a feeling of liberation. . . .

The feeling is not a feeling peculiar to exquisite or (perhaps, as better) precise realization, and hence confined to poets who exceed us in nature as they do in speech. There is nothing rare about it although it may extend to degrees of rarity. On the contrary, just as Bergson refers to the simpler representations of aspiration occurring in the lives of the saints, so we may refer to the simpler representations of an aspiration (not the same, yet not wholly unlike) occurring in the lives of those who have just written their first essential poems. After all, the young man or young woman who has written a few poems and who wants to read them is merely the voluble convert or the person looking in a mirror who sees suddenly the traces of an unexpected genealogy. We are interested in this transformation primarily on the part of the poet. Yet it is a thing that communicates itself to the reader. Anyone who has read a long poem day after day as, for example, *The Faerie Queene*, knows how the poem comes to possess the reader and how it naturalizes him in its own imagination and liberates him there.

This sense of liberation may be examined specifically in relation to the experience of writing a poem that completely accomplishes the purpose of the poet. Bergson had in mind religious aspiration. The poet who experiences what was once called inspiration experiences both aspiration and inspiration. But that is not a difference, for it is clear that Bergson intended to include in aspiration not only desire but the fulfillment of desire, not only the petition but the harmonious decree. What is true of the experience of the poet is no doubt true of the experience of the painter, of the musician and of any artist. If, then, when we speak of liberation, we mean an exodus; if when we speak of justification, we mean a kind of justice of which we had not known and on which we had not counted; if when we experience a sense of purification, we can think of the establishing of a self, it is certain that the experience of the poet is of no less a degree than the experience of the mystic and we may be certain that in the case of poets, the peers of saints, those experiences are of no less a degree than the experiences of the saints themselves. It is a question of the nature of the experience. It is not a question of identifying or relating dissimilar figures; that is to say, it is not a question of making saints out of poets or poets out of saints.

In this state of elevation we feel perfectly adapted to the idea that moves and *l'oiseau qui chante*. The identity of the feeling is subject to discussion and, from this, it follows that its value is debatable. It may be dismissed, on the one hand, as a commonplace aesthetic satisfaction; and, on the other hand, if we say that the idea of God is merely a poetic idea, even if the supreme poetic idea, and that our notions of heaven and hell are merely poetry not so called, even if poetry that involves us vitally, the feeling of deliverance, of a release, of a perfection touched, of a vocation so that all men may know the truth and that the truth may set them free—if we say these things and if we are able to see the poet who achieved God and placed Him in His seat in heaven in all His glory, the poet himself, still in the ecstasy of the poem that completely accomplished his purpose, would have seemed, whether young or old, whether in rags or ceremonial robe, a man who needed what he had created, uttering the hymns of joy that followed his creation. This may be a gross exaggeration of a very simple matter. But perhaps that remark is true of many of the more prodigious things of life and death.

5

The centuries have a way of being male. Without pretending to say whether they get this character from their good heroes or their bad ones, it is certain that they get it, in part, from their philosophers and poets. It is curious, looking back at them, to see how much of the impression that they leave has been derived from the progress of thought in their time and from the abundance of the arts, including poetry, left behind and how little of it comes from prouder and much noisier things. Thus, when we think of the seventeenth century, it is to be remarked how much of the strength of its appearance is associated with the idea that this was a time when the incredible suffered most at the hands of the credible. We think of it as a period of hard thinking. We have only their records and memories by which to recall such eras, not the sight and sound of those that lived in them preserved in an eternity of dust and dirt. When we look back at the face of the seventeenth century, it is at the rigorous face of the rigorous thinker and, say, the Miltonic image of a poet, severe and determined. In effect, what we are remembering is the rather haggard background of the incredible, the imagination without intelligence, from which a younger figure is emerging, stepping forward in the company of a muse of its own, still half-beast and somehow more than human, a kind of sister of the Minotaur. This younger figure is the intelligence that endures. It is the imagination of the son still bearing the antique imagination of the father. It is the clear intelligence of the young man still bearing the burden of the obscurities of the intelligence of the old. It is the spirit out of its own self, not out of some surrounding myth, delineating with accurate speech the complications of which it is composed. For this Aeneas, it is the past that is Anchises.

The incredible is not a part of poetic truth. On the contrary, what concerns us in poetry, as in everything else, is the belief of credible people in credible things. It follows that poetic truth is the truth of credible things, not so much that it is actually so, as that it must be so. It is toward that alone that it is possible for the intelligence to move. In one of his letters, Xavier Doudan says: "*Il y a longtemps que je pense que celui qui n'aurait que des idées claires serait assurément un sot.*" The reply to this is that it is impossible to conceive of a man who has nothing but clear ideas; for our nature is an illimitable space through which the intelligence moves without coming to an end. The incredible is inexhaustible but, fortunately, it is not always the same. We come, in this way, to understand that the moment of exaltation that the poet experiences when he writes a poem that completely accomplishes his purpose, is a moment of victory over the incredible, a moment of purity that does not become any the less pure because, as what was incredible is eliminated, something newly credible takes its place. As we come to the point at which it is necessary to be explicit in respect to poetic truth, note that, if we say that the philosopher pursues the truth in one way and the poet in another, it is implied that both are pursuing the same thing, and we overlook the fact that they are pursuing two different parts of a whole. It is as if we said that the end of logic, mathematics, physics, reason and imagination is all one. In short, it is as if we said that there is no difference between philosophic truth and poetic truth. There is a difference between them and it is the difference between logical and empirical knowledge. Since philosophers do not agree in respect to what constitutes philosophic truth, as Bertrand Russell (if any illustration whatever is necessary) demonstrates in his *Inquiry into Meaning and Truth*, even in the casual comment that truth as a static concept is to be discarded, it may not be of much use to improvise a definition of poetic truth. Nevertheless, it may be said that poetic truth is an agreement with reality, brought about by the imagination of a man disposed to be strongly influenced by his imagination, which he believes, for a time, to be true, expressed in terms of his emotions or, since it is less of a restriction to say so, in terms of his own personality. And so stated, the difference between philosophic truth and poetic truth appears to become final. As to the definition itself, it is an expedient for getting on. We shall come back to the nature of poetic truth very shortly.

In the most propitious climate and in the midst of life's virtues, the simple figure of the youth as virile poet is always surrounded by a cloud of double characters, against whose thought and speech it is imperative that he should remain on constant guard. These are the poetic philosophers and the philosophical poets. Mme. de Staël said: "*Nos meilleurs poètes lyriques, en France, ce sont peut-être nos grands prosateurs, Bossuet, Pascal, Féne-lon, Buffon, Jean-Jacques. . . .*" M. Claudel added Rabelais, Chateaubriand, even Balzac, and when he did so, M. René Fernandat said: "*On remarquera que M. Claudel a supprimé les 'peut-être' de Mme. de Staël.*" In English the poetic aspect of Bunyan is quite commonly recognized. This is an occasion to call attention to William Penn as an English poet, although he may never have written a line of verse. But the illustration of Descartes is irresistible. To speak of figures like Descartes as double characters is an inconceivable difficulty. In his exegesis of *The Discourse on Method*, Leon Roth says:

His vision showed him first the "dictionary," then the "poets," and only afterwards the est et non; and his "rationalism," like the "anti-rationalism" of Pascal, was the product of a struggle not always completely successful. What less "rationalistic" could there be than the early thought preserved by Baillet from the Olympica (one may note in passing the poetical names of all these early works): "There are sentences in the writings of the poets more serious than in those of the philosophers. . . . There are in us, as in a flint, seeds of knowledge. Philosophers adduce them through the reason; poets strike them out from the imagination, and these are the brighter." It was the "rationalist" Voltaire who first called attention to the "poetic" in Descartes. . . . To the casual *reader there is nothing more remarkable than the care-less richness of his style. It is full of similes drawn not only from the arts, like architecture, painting and the stage, but also from the familiar scenes of ordinary and country life. . . . And this not only in his early writing. It is apparent even in his latest published work, the sci-entific analysis of the "passions of the soul," and it was Voltaire again who commented first on the fact that the last thing from his pen was a ballet written for the Queen of Sweden.*

The philosopher proves that the philosopher exists. The poet merely enjoys existence. The philosopher thinks of the world as an enormous pastiche or, as he puts it, the world is as the percipient. Thus Kant says that the ob-jects of perception are conditioned by the nature of the mind as to their form. But the poet says that, whatever it may be, *la vie est plus belle que les idées*. One needs hardly to be told that men more or less irrational are only more or less rational; so that it was not surprising to find Raymond Mortimer saying in the *New Statesman* that the "thoughts" of Shakespeare or Raleigh or Spenser were in fact only contemporary commonplaces and that it was a Victorian habit to praise poets as thinkers, since their "thoughts are usually borrowed or confused." But do we come away from Shakespeare with the sense that we have been reading contemporary commonplaces? Long ago, Sarah Bernhardt was playing Hamlet. When she came to the soliloquy "To be or not to be," she half turned her back on the audience and slowly weaving one hand in a small circle above her head and regarding it, she said, with deliberation and as from the depths of a hallucination:

D'être ou ne pas d'être, c'est là la question . . .

and one followed her, lost in the intricate metamorphosis of thoughts that passed through the mind with a gallantry, an accuracy of abundance, a crowding and pressing of direction, which, for thoughts that were both borrowed and confused, cancelled the borrowing and obliterated the confusion.

There is a life apart from politics. It is this life that the youth as virile poet lives, in a kind of radiant and productive atmosphere. It is the life of that atmosphere. There the philosopher is an alien. The pleasure that the poet has there is a pleasure of agreement with the radiant and productive world in which he lives. It is an agreement that Mallarmé found in the sound of

Le vierge, le vivace et le bel aujourd'hui

and that Hopkins found in the color of

The thunder-purple seabeach plumèd purple-of-thunder.

The indirect purpose or, perhaps, it would be better to say, inverted effect of soliloquies in hell and of most celestial poems and, in a general sense, of all music played on the terraces of the audiences of the moon, seems to be to produce an agreement with reality. It is the *mundo* of the imagination in which the imaginative man delights and not the gaunt world of the reason. The pleasure is the pleasure of powers that create a truth that cannot be arrived at by the reason alone, a truth that the poet recognizes by sensation. The morality of the poet's radiant and productive atmosphere is the morality of the right sensation.

6

I have compared poetry and philosophy; I have made a point of the degree to which poetry is personal, both in its origin and in its end, and have spoken of the typical exhilaration that appears to be inseparable from genuine poetic activity; I have said that the general progress from the incredible to the credible was a progress in which poetry has participated; I have improvised a definition of poetic truth and have spoken of the integrity and peculiarity of the poetic character. Summed up, our position at the moment is that the poet must get rid of the hieratic in everything that concerns him and must move constantly in the direction of the credible. He must create his unreal out of what is real.

If we consider the nature of our experience when we are in agreement with reality, we find, for one thing, that we cease to be metaphysicians. William James said:

Most of them [i.e., metaphysicians] have been invalids. I am one, can't sleep, can't make a decision, can't buy a horse, can't do anything that befits a man; and yet you say from my photograph that I must be a second General Sherman, only greater and better! All right! I love you for the fond delusion.

For all the reasons stated by William James, and for many more, and in spite of M. Jacques Maritain, we do not want to be metaphysicians. In the crowd around the simple figure of the youth as virile poet, there are metaphysicians, among the others. And having ceased to be metaphysicians, even though we have acquired something from them as from all men, and standing in the radiant and productive atmosphere, and examining first one detail of that world, one particular, and then another, as we find them by chance, and observing many things that seem to be poetry without any intervention on our part, as, for example, the blue sky, and noting, in any case, that the imagination never brings anything into the world but that, on the contrary, like the personality of the poet in the act of creating, it is no more than a process, and desiring with all the power of our desire not to write falsely, do we not begin to think of the possibility that poetry is only reality, after all, and that poetic truth is a factual truth, seen, it may be, by those whose range in the perception of fact—that is, whose sensibility—is greater than our own? From that point of view, the truth that we experience when we are in agreement with reality is the truth of fact. In consequence, when men, baffled by philosophic truth, turn to poetic truth, they return to their starting-point, they return to fact, not, it ought to be clear, to bare fact (or call it absolute fact), but to fact possibly beyond their perception in the first instance and outside the normal range of their sensibility. What we have called elevation and elation on the part of the poet, which he communicates to the reader, may be not so much elevation as an incandescence of the intelligence and so more than ever a triumph over the incredible. Here as part of the purification that all of us undergo as we approach any central purity, and that we feel in its presence, we can say:

No longer do I believe that there is a mystic muse, sister of the Minotaur. This is another of the monsters I had for nurse, whom I have wasted. I am myself a part of what is real, and it is my own speech and the strength of it, this only, that I hear or ever shall.

These words may very well be an inscription above the portal to what lies ahead. But if poetic truth means fact and if fact includes the whole of it as it is between the extreme poles of sensibility, we are talking about a thing as extensible as it is ambiguous. We have excluded absolute fact as an element of poetic truth. But this has been done arbitrarily and with a sense of absolute fact as fact destitute of any imaginative aspect whatever. Unhappily the more destitute it becomes the more it begins to be precious. We must limit ourselves to saying that there are so many things which, as they are, and without any intervention of the imagination, seem to be imaginative objects that it is no doubt true that absolute fact includes everything that the imagination includes. This is our intimidating thesis.

One sees demonstrations of this everywhere. For example, if we close our eyes and think of a place where it would be pleasant to spend a holiday, and if there slide across the black eyes, like a setting on a stage, a rock that sparkles, a blue sea that lashes, and hemlocks in which the sun can merely fumble, this inevitably demonstrates, since the rock and sea, the wood and sun are those that have been familiar to us in Maine, that much of the world of fact is the equivalent of the world of the imagination, because it looks like it. Here we are on the border of the question of the relationship of the imagination and memory, which we avoid. It is important to believe that the visible is the equivalent of the invisible; and once we believe it, we have destroyed the imagination; that is to say, we have destroyed the false imagination, the false conception of the imagination as some incalculable *vates* within us, unhappy Rodomontade. One is often tempted to say that the best definition of poetry is that poetry is the sum of its attributes. So, here, we may say that the best definition of true imagination is that it is the sum of our faculties. Poetry is the scholar's art. The acute intelligence of the imagination, the illimitable resources of its memory, its power to possess the moment it perceives—if we were speaking of light itself, and thinking of the relationship between objects and light, no further demonstration would be necessary. Like light, it adds nothing, except itself. What light requires a day to do, and by day I mean a kind of Biblical revolution of time, the imagination does in the twinkling of an eye. It colors, increases, brings to a beginning and end, invents languages, crushes men and, for that matter, gods in its hands, it says to women more than it is possible to say, it rescues all of us from what we have called absolute fact and while it does these things, and more, it makes sure that

> . . . *la mandoline jase,*
> *Parmi les frissons de brise.*

Having identified poetic truth as the truth of fact, since fact includes poetic fact, that is to say: the indefinite number of actual things that are indistinguishable from objects of the imagination; and having, as we hope, washed the imagination clean, we may now return, once again, to the figure of the youth as virile poet and join him, or try to do so, in coming to the decision, on which, for him and for us, too, so much depends. At what level of the truth shall he compose his poems? That is the question on which he is reflecting, as he sits in the radiant and productive atmosphere, which is his life, surrounded not only by double characters and metaphysicians, but by many men and many kinds of men, by many women and many children and many kinds of women and of children. The question concerns the function of the poet today and tomorrow, but makes no pretence beyond. He is able to read the inscription on the portal and he repeats:

*I am myself a part of what is real and it is my own
speech and the strength of it, this only, that I hear or ever
shall.*

He says, so that we can all hear him:

*I am the truth, since I am part of what is real, but
neither more nor less than those around me. And I am
imagination, in a leaden time and in a world that does not
move for the weight of its own heaviness.*

Can there be the slightest doubt what the decision will
be? Can we suppose for a moment that he will be con-
tent merely to make notes, merely to copy Katahdin,
when, with his sense of the heaviness of the world, he
feels his own power to lift, or help to lift, that heaviness
away? Can we think that he will elect anything except
to exercise his power to the full and at its height, mean-
ing by this as part of what is real, to rely on his imagina-
tion, to make his own imagination that of those who have
none, or little?

And how will he do this? It is not possible to say how
an imaginative person will do a thing. Having made an
election, he will be faithful to the election that he has
made. Having elected to exercise his power to the full
and at its height, and having identified his power as the
power of the imagination, he may begin its exercise by
studying it in exercise and proceed little by little, as he
becomes his own master, to those violences which are

the maturity of his desires. The character of the crisis through which we are passing today, the reason why we live in a leaden time, was summed up in a note on Klaus Mann's recent book on Gide, as follows:

The main problem which Gide tries to solve—the crisis of our time—is the reconciliation of the inalienable rights of the individual to personal development and the necessity for the diminution of the misery of the masses.

When the poet has converted this into his own terms: the figure of the youth as virile poet and the community growing day by day more and more colossal, the consciousness of his function, if he is a serious artist, is a measure of his obligation. And so is the consciousness of his history. In the *Reflections on History* of Jakob Burckhardt, there are some pages of notes on the historical consideration of poetry. Burckhardt thought (citing Schopenhauer and Aristotle) that poetry achieves more for the knowledge of human nature than history. Burckhardt considers the status of poetry at various epochs, among various peoples and classes, asking each time *who* is singing or writing, and for *whom.* Poetry is the voice of religion, prophecy, mythology, history, national life and inexplicably, for him, of literature. He says:

It is a matter for great surprise that Virgil, in those circumstances, could occupy his high rank, could dominate all the age which followed and become a mythical figure. How infinitely great are the gradations of existence from the epic rhapsodist to the novelist of today!

This was written seventy-five years ago. The present generation of poets is not accustomed to measure itself by obligations of such weight nor to think of itself as Burckhardt seems to have thought of epic bards or, to choose another example at random, of the writers of hymns, for he speaks of "the Protestant hymn as the supreme religious expression, especially of the seventeenth century."

The poet reflecting on his course, which is the same thing as a reflection by him and by us, on the course of poetry, will decide to do as the imagination bids, because he has no choice, if he is to remain a poet. Poetry is the imagination of life. A poem is a particular of life thought of for so long that one's thought has become an inseparable part of it or a particular of life so intensely felt that the feeling has entered into it. When, therefore, we say that the world is a compact of real things so like the unreal things of the imagination that they are indistinguishable from one another and when, by way of illustration, we cite, say, the blue sky, we can be sure that the thing cited is always something that, whether by thinking or feeling, has become a part of our vital experience of life, even though we are not aware of it. It is easy to suppose that few people realize on that occasion, which comes to all of us, when we look at the blue sky for the first time, that is to say: not merely see it, but look at it and experience it and for the first time have a sense that we live in the center of a physical poetry, a geography that would be intolerable except for the non-geography that exists there

—few people realize that they are looking at the world of their own thoughts and the world of their own feelings. On that occasion, the blue sky is a particular of life that we have thought of often, even though unconsciously, and that we have felt intensely in those crystallizations of freshness that we no more remember than we remember this or that gust of wind in spring or autumn. The experiences of thinking and feeling accumulate particularly in the abnormal ranges of sensibility; so that, to use a bit of M. Focillon's personal language, while the "normative type" of poet is likely to be concerned with pretty much the same facts as those with which the genius, or, rather, the youth as virile poet, is concerned, the genius, because of the abnormal ranges of his sensibility, not only accumulates experiences with greater rapidity, but accumulates experiences and qualities of experience accessible only in the extreme ranges of sensibility.

But genius is not our concern. We are trying to define what we mean by the imagination of life, and, in addition, by that special illumination, special abundance and severity of abundance, virtue in the midst of indulgence and order in disorder that is involved in the idea of virility. We have been referring constantly to the simple figure of the youth, in his character of poet, as virile poet. The reason for this is that if, for the poet, the imagination is paramount, and if he dwells apart in his imagination, as the philosopher dwells in his reason, and as the priest dwells in his belief, the masculine nature that we propose for one that must be the master of our lives will be lost as, for example, in the folds of the garments of the ghost or ghosts of Aristotle. As we say these things, there begins to develop, in addition to the figure that has been seated in our midst, composed, in the radiant and productive atmosphere with which we have surrounded him, an intimation of what he is thinking as he reflects on the imagination of life, determined to be its master and ours. He is thinking of those facts of experience of which all of us have thought and which all of us have felt with such intensity, and he says:

Inexplicable sister of the Minotaur, enigma and mask, although I am part of what is real, hear me and recognize me as part of the unreal. I am the truth but the truth of that imagination of life in which with unfamiliar motion and manner you guide me in those exchanges of speech in which your words are mine, mine yours.

III

Three Academic Pieces

I

THE ACCURACY of accurate letters is an accuracy
with respect to the structure of reality.

Thus, if we desire to formulate an accurate theory of
poetry, we find it necessary to examine the structure of
reality, because reality is the central reference for poetry.
By way of accomplishing this, suppose we examine one
of the significant components of the structure of reality—
that is to say, the resemblance between things.

First, then, as to the resemblance between things in
nature, it should be observed that resemblance consti-
tutes a relation between them since, in some sense, all
things resemble each other. Take, for example, a beach
extending as far as the eye can reach, bordered, on the
one hand, by trees and, on the other, by the sea. The sky
is cloudless and the sun is red. In what sense do the ob-
jects in this scene resemble each other? There is enough
green in the sea to relate it to the palms. There is enough
of the sky reflected in the water to create a resemblance,
in some sense, between them. The sand is yellow be-
tween the green and the blue. In short, the light alone
creates a unity not only in the recedings of distance,
where differences become invisible, but also in the con-
tacts of closer sight. So, too, sufficiently generalized, each

man resembles all other men, each woman resembles all other women, this year resembles last year. The beginning of time will, no doubt, resemble the end of time. One world is said to resemble another.

A moment ago the resemblance between things was spoken of as one of the significant components of the structure of reality. It is significant because it creates the relation just described. It binds together. It is the base of appearance. In nature, however, the relation is between two or more of the parts of reality. In metaphor (and this word is used as a symbol for the single aspect of poetry with which we are now concerned—that is to say, the creation of resemblance by the imagination, even though metamorphosis might be a better word)—in metaphor, the resemblance may be, first, between two or more parts of reality; second, between something real and something imagined or, what is the same thing, between something imagined and something real as, for example, between music and whatever may be evoked by it; and, third, between two imagined things as when we say that God is good, since the statement involves a resemblance between two concepts, a concept of God and a concept of goodness.

We are not dealing with identity. Both in nature and in metaphor identity is the vanishing-point of resemblance. After all, if a man's exact double entered a room, seated himself and spoke the words that were in the man's mind, it would remain a resemblance. James Wardrop, in *Signature*, said recently:

The business of the press is to furnish an indefinite public with a potentially indefinite number of identical texts.

Nature is not mechanical to that extent for all its mornings and evenings, for all its inhabitants of China or India or Russia, for all its waves, or its leaves, or its hands. Its prodigy is not identity but resemblance and its universe of reproduction is not an assembly line but an incessant creation. Because this is so in nature, it is so in metaphor.

Nor are we dealing with imitation. The difference between imitation and resemblance is a nicety. An imitation may be described as an identity manqué. It is artificial. It is not fortuitous as a true metaphor is. If it is an imitation of something in nature, it may even surpass identity and assume a praeter-nature. It may very well escape the derogatory. If it is an imitation of something in metaphor, it is lifeless and that, finally, is what is wrong with it. Resemblance in metaphor is an activity of the imagination; and in metaphor the imagination is life. In Chinese metaphor, there is a group of subjects to which poets used to address themselves, just as early Western painters and etchers used to address themselves to such a subject as the Virgin crowned by Angels. The variations in these themes were not imitations, nor identities, but resemblances.

In reality, there is a level of resemblance, which is the level of nature. In metaphor, there is no such level. If there were it would be the level of resemblance of the imagination, which has no such level. If, to our surprise, we should meet a monsieur who told us that he was from another world, and if he had in fact all the indicia of divinity, the luminous body, the nimbus, the heraldic stigmata, we should recognize him as above the level of nature but not as above the level of the imagination. So, too, if, to our surprise, we should meet one of these morons whose remarks are so conspicuous a part of the folk-lore of the world of the radio—remarks made without using either the tongue or the brain, spouted much like the spoutings of small whales—we should recognize him as below the level of nature but not as below the level of the imagination. It is not, however, a question of above or below but simply of beyond. Level is an abbreviated form of level of resemblance. The statement that the imagination has no level of resemblance is not to be taken as a statement that the imagination itself has no limits. The imagination is deceptive in this respect. There is a limit to its power to surpass resemblance and that limit is to be found in nature. The imagination is able to manipulate nature as by creating three legs and five arms but it is not able to create a totally new nature as, for instance, a new element with creatures indigenous thereto, their costumes and cuisines. Any discussion of level is a discussion of balance as well. Thus, a false exaggeration is a disturbing of the balance between reality and the imagination.

Resemblances between one object and another as between one brick and another, one egg and another, are elementary. There are many objects which in respect to what they suggest resemble other objects and we may include here, as objects, people. Thus, in addition to the fact that one man resembles all other men, something about one man may make him resemble some other particular man and this is true even when the something about him is detached from him, as his wig. The wig of a particular man reminds us of some other particular man and resembles him. A strand of a child's hair brings back the whole child and in that way resembles the child. There must be vast numbers of things within this category. Apparently objects of sentiment most easily prove the existence of this kind of resemblance: something in a locket, one's grandfather's high beaver hat, one's grandmother's hand-woven blankets. One may find intimations of immortality in an object on the mantelpiece; and these intimations are as real in the mind in which they occur as the mantelpiece itself. Even if they are only a part of an adult make-believe, the whole point is that the structure of reality because of the range of resemblances that it contains is measurably an adult make-believe. Perhaps the whole field of connotation is based on resemblance. Perhaps resemblance which seems to be related so closely to the imagination is related even more closely to the intelligence, of which perceptions of resemblance are effortless accelerations.

What has just been said shows that there are private resemblances. The resemblance of the baby's shoes to the baby, by suggestion, is likely to be a resemblance that exists for one or two alone. A public resemblance, by contrast, like the resemblance of the profile of a mountain to the profile of General Washington, exists for that great class of people who co-exist with the great ferns in public gardens, amplified music and minor education. What our eyes behold may well be the text of life but one's meditations on the text and the disclosures of these meditations are no less a part of the structure of reality.

It quite seems as if there is an activity that makes one thing resemble another (possibly as a phase of the police power of conformity). What the eye beholds may be the text of life. It is, nevertheless, a text that we do not write. The eye does not beget in resemblance. It sees. But the mind begets in resemblance as the painter begets in representation; that is to say, as the painter makes his world within a world; or as the musician begets in music, in the obvious small pieces having to do with gardens in the rain or the fountains of Rome and in the obvious larger pieces having to do with the sea, Brazilian night or those woods in the neighborhood of Vienna in which the hunter was accustomed to blow his horn and in which, also, yesterday, the birds sang preludes to the atom bomb. It is not difficult, having once predicated such an activity, to attribute it to a desire for resemblance. What a ghastly situation it would be if the world of the dead was actually different from the world of the living and, if as life ends, instead of passing to a former Victorian sphere, we passed into a land in which none of our problems had been solved, after all, and nothing resembled anything we have ever known and nothing resembled anything else in shape, in color, in sound, in look or otherwise. To say farewell to our generation and to look forward to a continuation in a Jerusalem of pure surrealism would account for the taste for oblivion.

The study of the activity of resemblance is an approach to the understanding of poetry. Poetry is a satisfying of the desire for resemblance. As the mere satisfying of a desire, it is pleasurable. But poetry if it did nothing but satisfy a desire would not rise above the level of many lesser things. Its singularity is that in the act of satisfying the desire for resemblance it touches the sense of reality, it enhances the sense of reality, heightens it, intensifies it. If resemblance is described as a partial similarity between two dissimilar things, it complements and reinforces that which the two dissimilar things have in common. It makes it brilliant. When the similarity is between things of adequate dignity, the resemblance may be said to transfigure or to sublimate them. Take, for example, the resemblance between reality and any projection of it in belief or in metaphor. What is it that these two have in common? Is not the glory of the idea of any future state a relation between a present and a future glory? The brilliance of earth is the brilliance of every paradise. However, not all poetry attempts such grandiose transfiguration. Everyone can call to mind a variety of figures and see clearly how these resemblances please and why; how inevitably they heighten our sense of reality. The images in Ecclesiastes:

*Or ever
the silver cord be loosed, or the golden bowl be broken,
or the pitcher be broken at the fountain, or the wheel
broken at the cistern—*

these images are not the language of reality, they are the
symbolic language of metamorphosis, or resemblance, of
poetry, but they relate to reality and they intensify our
sense of it and they give us the pleasure of "lentor and
solemnity" in respect to the most commonplace objects.
These images have a special interest, as a group of im-
ages in harmony with each other. In both prose and po-
etry, images come willingly but, usually, although there
is a relation between the subject of the images there is no
relation between the images themselves. A group of im-
ages in harmony with each other would constitute a poem
within, or above, a poem. The suggestion sounds euphu-
istic. If the desire for resemblance is the desire to enjoy
reality, it may be no less true that the desire to enjoy
reality, an acute enough desire today, is the desire for
elegance. Euphuism had its origin in the desire for ele-
gance and it was euphuism that was a reason in the sun
for metaphor. A school of literary ascetics denying itself
any indulgence in resemblances would, necessarily, fall
back on reality and vent all its relish there. The meta-
phorical school, in the end, does the same thing.

The proliferation of resemblances extends an object.
The point at which this process begins, or rather at
which this growth begins, is the point at which am-

biguity has been reached. The ambiguity that is so fa-
vorable to the poetic mind is precisely the ambiguity
favorable to resemblance. In this ambiguity, the inten-
sification of reality by resemblance increases realization
and this increased realization is pleasurable. It is as if a
man who lived indoors should go outdoors on a day of
sympathetic weather. His realization of the weather
would exceed that of a man who lives outdoors. It might,
in fact, be intense enough to convert the real world about
him into an imagined world. In short, a sense of reality
keen enough to be in excess of the normal sense of
reality creates a reality of its own. Here what matters
is that the intensification of the sense of reality creates
a resemblance: that reality of its own is a reality. This
may be going round a circle, first clockwise, then anti-
clockwise. If the savor of life is the savor of reality,
the fact will establish itself whichever way one ap-
proaches it.

The relations between the ego and reality must be left
largely on the margin. Yet Narcissus did not expect,
when he looked in the stream, to find in his hair a
serpent coiled to strike, nor, when he looked in his own
eyes there, to be met by a look of hate, nor, in general,
to discover himself at the center of an inexplicable ugli-
ness from which he would be bound to avert himself. On
the contrary, he sought out his image everywhere be-
cause it was the principle of his nature to do so and, to
go a step beyond that, because it was the principle of his
nature, as it is of ours, to expect to find pleasure in what

he found. Narcissism, then, involves something beyond
the prime sense of the word. It involves, also, this prin-
ciple, that as we seek out our resemblances we expect
to find pleasure in doing so; that is to say, in what we
find. So strong is that expectation that we find nothing
else. What is true of the observations of ourselves is
equally true of the observations of resemblances be-
tween other things having no relation to us. We say
that the sea, when it expands in a calm and immense re-
flection of the sky, resembles the sky, and this statement
gives us pleasure. We enjoy the resemblance for the
same reason that, if it were possible to look into the sea as
into glass and if we should do so and suddenly should
behold there some extraordinary transfiguration of our-
selves, the experience would strike us as one of those
amiable revelations that nature occasionally vouchsafes
to favorites. So, when we think of arpeggios, we think of
opening wings and the effect of the resemblance is pleas-
urable. When we read Ecclesiastes the effect of the sym-
bols is pleasurable because as symbols they are resem-
blances and as resemblances they are pleasurable and
they are pleasurable because it is a principle of our nature
that they should be, the principle being not something
derived from Narcissism since Narcissism itself is merely
an evidence of the operation of the principle that we ex-
pect to find pleasure in resemblances.

We have been trying to get at a truth about poetry, to
get at one of the principles that compose the theory of

poetry. It comes to this, that poetry is a part of the struc-
ture of reality. If this has been demonstrated, it pretty
much amounts to saying that the structure of poetry and
the structure of reality are one or, in effect, that poetry
and reality are one, or should be. This may be less thesis
than hypothesis. Yet hypotheses relating to poetry, al-
though they may appear to be very distant illuminations,
could be the fires of fate, if rhetoric ever meant anything.

There is a gradus ad Metaphoram. The nature of a
metaphor is, like the nature of a play, comic, tragic,
tragic-comic and so on. It may be poetic. A poetic meta-
phor—that is to say, a metaphor poetic in a sense more
specific than the sense in which poetry and metaphor are
one—appears to be poetry at its source. It is. At least
it is poetry at one of its sources although not necessarily
the most fecundating. But the steps to this particular
abstraction, the gradus ad Metaphoram in respect to the
general sense in which poetry and metaphor are one, are,
like the ascent to any of the abstractions that interest
us importantly, an ascent through illusion which gathers
round us more closely and thickly, as we might expect it
to do, the more we penetrate it.

In the fewest possible words since, as between resem-
blances, one is always a little more nearly perfect than
another and since, from this, it is easy for perfectionism
of a sort to evolve, it is not too extravagant to think of
resemblances and of the repetitions of resemblances as
a source of the ideal. In short, metaphor has its aspect of

the ideal. This aspect of it cannot be dismissed merely because we think that we have long since outlived the ideal. The truth is that we are constantly outliving it and yet the ideal itself remains alive with an enormous life.

Three Academic Pieces

2

SOMEONE PUTS A PINEAPPLE TOGETHER

I

O juventes, O filii, he contemplates
A wholly artificial nature, in which
The profusion of metaphor has been increased.

It is something on a table that he sees,
The root of a form, as of this fruit, a fund,
The angel at the center of this rind,

This husk of Cuba, tufted emerald,
Himself, may be, the irreducible X
At the bottom of imagined artifice,

Its inhabitant and elect expositor.
It is as if there were three planets: the sun,
The moon and the imagination, or, say,

Day, night and man and his endless effigies.
If he sees an object on a table, much like
A jar of the shoots of an infant country, green

And bright, or like a venerable urn,
Which, from the ash within it, fortifies
A green that is the ash of what green is,

He sees it in this tangent of himself.
And in this tangent it becomes a thing
Of weight, on which the weightless rests: from which

The ephemeras of the tangent swarm, the chance
Concourse of planetary originals,
Yet, as it seems, of human residence.

II

He must say nothing of the fruit that is
Not true, nor think it, less. He must defy
The metaphor that murders metaphor.

He seeks as image a second of the self,
Made subtle by truth's most jealous subtlety,
Like the true light of the truest sun, the true

Power in the waving of the wand of the moon,
Whose shining is the intelligence of our sleep.
He seeks an image certain as meaning is

To sound, sound's substance and executant,
The particular tingle in a proclamation
That makes it say the little thing it says,

Below the prerogative jumble. The fruit so seen
As a part of the nature that he contemplates
Is fertile with more than changes of the light

On the table or in the colors of the room.
Its propagations are more erudite,
Like precious scholia jotted down in the dark

Did not the age that bore him bear him among
Its infiltrations? There had been an age
When a pineapple on the table was enough,

Without the forfeit scholar coming in,
Without his enlargings and pale arrondissements,
Without the furious roar in his capital.

Green had, those days, its own implacable sting.
But now a habit of the truth had formed
To protect him in a privacy, in which

The scholar, captious, told him what he could
Of there, where the truth was not the respect of one,
But always of many things. He had not to be told

Of the incredible subjects of poetry.
He was willing they should remain incredible,
Because the incredible, also, has its truth,

Its tuft of emerald that is real, for all
Its invitation to false metaphor.
The incredible gave him a purpose to believe.

III

How thick this gobbet is with overlays,
The double fruit of boisterous epicures,
Like the same orange repeating on one tree

A single self. Divest reality
Of its propriety. Admit the shaft
Of that third planet to the table and then:

1. The hut stands by itself beneath the palms.
2. Out of their bottle the green genii come.
3. A vine has climbed the other side of the wall.

4. The sea is spouting upward out of rocks.
5. The symbol of feasts and of oblivion . . .
6. White sky, pink sun, trees on a distant peak.

7. These lozenges are nailed-up lattices.
8. The owl sits humped. It has a hundred eyes.
9. The coconut and cockerel in one.

10. This is how yesterday's volcano looks.
11. There is an island Palahude by name—
12. An uncivil shape like a gigantic haw.

These casual exfoliations are
Of the tropic of resemblance, sprigs
Of Capricorn or as the sign demands,

Apposites, to the slightest edge, of the whole
Undescribed composition of the sugar-cone,
Shiftings of an inchoate crystal tableau,

The momentary footings of a climb
Up the pineapple, a table Alp and yet
An Alp, a purple Southern mountain bisqued

With the molten mixings of related things,
Cat's taste possibly or possibly Danish lore,
The small luxuriations that portend

Universal delusions of universal grandeurs,
The slight incipiencies, of which the form,
At last, is the pineapple on the table or else

An object the sum of its complications, seen
And unseen. This is everybody's world.
Here the total artifice reveals itself

As the total reality. Therefore it is
One says even of the odor of this fruit,
That steeps the room, quickly, then not at all,

It is more than the odor of this core of earth
And water. It is that which is distilled
In the prolific ellipses that we know,

In the planes that tilt hard revelations on
The eye, a geometric glitter, tiltings
As of sections collecting toward the greenest cone.

3

OF IDEAL TIME AND CHOICE

Since thirty mornings are required to make
A day of which we say, this is the day
That we desired, a day of blank, blue wheels,

Involving the four corners of the sky,
Lapised and lacqued and freely emeraldine
In the space it fills, the silent motioner

There, of clear, revolving crystalline;
Since thirty summers are needed for a year
And thirty years, in the galaxies of birth,

Are time for counting and remembering,
And fill the earth with young men centuries old
And old men, who have chosen, and are cold

Because what they have chosen is their choice
No more and because they lack the will to tell
A matin gold from gold of Hesperus

The dot, the pale pole of resemblances
Experienced yet not well seen; of how
Much choosing is the final choice made up,

And who shall speak it, what child or wanderer
Or woman weeping in a room or man,
The last man given for epitome,

Upon whose lips the dissertation sounds,
And in what place, what exultant terminal,
And at what time both of the year and day;

And what heroic nature of what text
Shall be the celebration in the words
Of that oration, the happiest sense in which

A world agrees, thought's compromise, resolved
At last, the center of resemblance, found
Under the bones of time's philosophers?

The orator will say that we ourselves
Stand at the center of ideal time,
The inhuman making choice of a human self.

About One of

Marianne Moore's Poems

M‌Y PURPOSE is to bring together one of Miss Moore's poems and a paper, "On Poetic Truth," by H. D. Lewis. The poem, "He 'Digesteth Harde Yron,' " has just been reprinted in the *Partisan Reader*. The paper is to be found in the July number (1946) of *Philosophy, the Journal of the British Institute of Philosophy* (Macmillan, London).

I

Mr. Lewis begins by saying that poetry has to do with reality in its most individual aspect. An isolated fact, cut loose from the universe, has no significance for the poet. It derives its significance from the reality to which it belongs. To see things in their true perspective, we require to draw very extensively upon experiences that are past. All that we see and hear is given a meaning in this way. There is in reality an aspect of individuality at which every form of rational explanation stops short. Now, in his *Euphues*, Lyly repeats the following bit of folk-lore:

> *Let them both remember that the Estridge digesteth harde yron to preserve his health.*

The "Estridge," then, is the subject of Miss Moore's poem. In the second stanza she says:

> This bird watches his chicks with
> a maternal concentration, after
>   he has sat on the eggs
>   at night six weeks, his legs
> their only weapon of defense.

The *Encyclopaedia Britannica* says of the ostrich:

Extremely fleet of foot, when brought to bay the ostrich uses its strong legs with great effect. Several hens combine to lay their eggs in one nest, and on these the cock sits by night, while the females relieve one another by day.

Somehow, there is a difference between Miss Moore's bird and the bird of the *Encyclopaedia*. This difference grows when she describes her bird as

> The friend
> of hippotigers and wild
>   asses, it is as
>   though schooled by them he was
>
> the best of the unflying
> pegasi.

The difference signalizes a transition from one reality to another. It is the reality of Miss Moore that is the individual reality. That of the *Encyclopaedia* is the reality of isolated fact. Miss Moore's reality is significant. An aesthetic integration is a reality.

Nowhere in the poem does she speak directly of the subject of the poem by its name. She calls it "the camel-sparrow" and "the large sparrow Xenophon saw walking by a stream," "the bird," "quadruped-like bird" and

> *alert gargantuan*
> *little-winged, magnificently*
> *speedy running-bird.*

This, too, marks a difference. To confront fact in its total bleakness is for any poet a completely baffling experience. Reality is not the thing but the aspect of the thing. At first reading, this poem has an extraordinarily factual appearance. But it is, after all, an abstraction. Mr. Lewis says that for Plato the only reality that mattered is exemplified best for us in the principles of mathematics. The aim of our lives should be to draw ourselves away as much as possible from the unsubstantial, fluctuating facts of the world about us and establish some communion with the objects which are apprehended by thought and not sense. This was the source of Plato's asceticism. To the extent that Miss Moore finds only allusion tolerable she shares that asceticism. While she shares it she does so only as it may be necessary for her to do so in order to establish a particular reality or, better, a reality of her own particulars: the "overt" reality of Mr. Lewis. Take, for example, her particulars of the bird's egg. She says:

> *The egg piously shown*
> *as Leda's very own*
> *from which Castor and Pollux hatched,*
> *was an ostrich-egg.*

Again she speaks of

> *jewel-*
> *gorgeous ugly egg-shell*
> *goblet.*

It is obvious from these few quotations that Miss Moore has already found an individual reality in the ostrich and again in its egg. After all, it is the subject in poetry that releases the energy of the poet.

Mr. Lewis says that poetry has to do with matter that is foreign and alien. It is never familiar to us in the way in which Plato wished the conquests of the mind to be familiar. On the contrary its function, the need which it meets and which has to be met in some way in every age that is not to become decadent or barbarous, is precisely this contact with reality as it impinges upon us from outside, the sense that we can touch and feel a solid reality which does not wholly dissolve itself into the conceptions of our own minds. It is the individual and particular that does this. No fact is a bare fact, no individual fact is a universe in itself. Is not Miss Moore creating or finding and revealing some such reality in the stanza that follows?

> *Six hundred ostrich-brains served*
> *at one banquet, the ostrich-plume-tipped tent*
> > *and desert spear . . .*
> > > *eight pairs of ostriches*
> *in harness, dramatize a*
> > *meaning always missed*
> > *by the externalist.*

Here the sparrow-camel is all pomp and ceremony, a part of justice of which it was not only the symbol, as Miss Moore says, but also the source of its panoply and the delicacy of its feasts; that is to say, a part of unprecedented experience.

Miss Moore's finical phraseology is an element in her procedure. These lines illustrate this:

> *Although the sepyornis*
> *or roc that lives in Madagascar, and*
> > *the moa are extinct*

and

> *Heroism is exhausting.*

But what irrevocably detaches her from the *Encyclopaedia* is the irony of the following:

> *How*
> *could he, prized for plumes and eggs and young, used*
> > *even as a riding-*
> *beast, respect men hiding*

> *actorlike in ostrich-skins, with*
> *the right hand making the neck move*
> > *as if alive and*
> > *from a bag the left hand*
>
> *strewing grain, that ostriches*
> *might be decoyed and killed!*

and the delighted observation of the following:

> *whose comic duckling head on its*
> *great neck, revolves with compass-*
> > *needle nervousness,*
> > *when he stands guard, in S-*
>
> *like foragings as he is*
> *preening the down on his leaden-skinned back.*

The gist of the poem is that the camel-sparrow has escaped the greed that has led to the extinction of other birds linked to it in size, by its solicitude for its own welfare and that of its chicks. Considering the great purposes that poetry must serve, the interest of the poem is not in its meaning but in this, that it illustrates the achieving of an individual reality. Mr. Lewis has some very agreeable things to say about meaning. He says that the extraction of a meaning from a poem and appraisement of it by rational standards of truth have mainly been due to enthusiasm for moral or religious truth. He protests against the abstraction of this content from the whole and appraisement of it by other than aesthetic standards. The "something said" is important, but it is important for the poem only in so far as the saying of that particular something in a special way is a revelation of reality. He says:

If I am right, the essence of art is insight of a special kind into reality.

Moreover, if he is right, the question as to Miss Moore's poem is not in respect to its meaning but in respect to its potency as a work of art. Does it make us so aware of the reality with which it is concerned, because of the poignancy and penetration of the poet, that it forces something upon our consciousness? The reality so imposed need not be a great reality.

Of course, if it does, it serves our purpose quite as certainly as a less modest poem would serve it. It is here, Mr. Lewis concludes, that the affinity of art and religion is most evident today. He says that both have to mediate for us a reality not ourselves and that this is what the poet does and that the supreme virtue here is humility, for the humble are they that move about the world with the lure of the real in their hearts.

2

Life, not the artist, creates or reveals reality: time and experience in the poet, in the painter. During this last September, I visited the old Zeller house in the Tulpehocken, in Pennsylvania. This family of religious refugees came to this country in 1709, lived for some fifteen or twenty years in the Scoharie region in New York and then went down the Susquehanna to the valley in which the house was built. Over the door there is an architectural cartouche of the cross with palm-branches below, placed there, no doubt, to indicate that the house and those that lived in it were consecrated to the glory of God. From this doorway they faced the hills that were part of the frame of their valley, the familiar shelter in which they spent their laborious lives, happy in the faith and worship in which they rejoiced. Their reality consisted of both the visible and the invisible. On another occasion, a man went with me to visit Christ Church near Stouchsburg. This stout old Lutheran felt about his church very much as the Irish are said to feel about God. Kate O'Brien says that in Ireland God is a member of the family. The man told me that last spring a scovy duck had built her nest in the chimney of the church. When, finally, her brood was hatched, the ducklings came out of a stove in one of the rooms in the basement of the church. There were six of them and they are alive today on the sexton's farm. When the committee of the church in charge of the building was making its plans last spring, this true lover of his church agreed to paint the fence around the adjoining graveyard. In part, this fence consisted of cast-iron spears. He painted the spear-head silver and the staves black, one by one, week after week, until the job was done. Yet obviously this man's reality is the church-building but as a fellow-existence, of a sort.

. . .

As we drove along the road, we met one of the Lutheran's friends, who had been leader of the choir in Trinity Tulpehocken Reformed Church for more than a generation. He had wrapped his throat up in flannel because, he said, one of his tendons was sore. At choir-practice the night before, the hymns for the Sunday service had been selected. He was on his way to the church to put the numbers in the rack. When he had done this, he went with us to the old graveyard of this church. This was an enclosure of about an acre, possibly a little more. The wall was of limestone about four feet high, weather-beaten, barren, bald. In the graveyard were possibly eight or ten sheep, the color of the wall and of many of the gravestones and even of some of the tufts of grass, bleached and silvery in the hard sunlight. The droppings of the sheep fertilized the soil. There were a few cedars here and there but these only accentuated the sense of abandonment and destitution, the sense that, after all, the vast mausoleum of human memory is emptier than one had supposed. Near by stood the manse, also of limestone, apparently vacant, the upper part of each window white with the half-drawn blind, the lower part black with the vacantness of the place. Although the two elderly men were in a way a diversion from the solitude, there could not be any effective diversion from the reality that time and experience had created here, the desolation that penetrated one like something final. Later, when I had returned to New York, I went to the exhibition of books in the Morgan Library held by the American Institute of Graphic Arts. The brilliant pages from Poland, France, Finland and so on, books of tales, of poetry, of folk-lore, were as if the barren reality that I had just experienced had suddenly taken color, become alive and from a single thing become many things and people, vivid, active, intently trying out a thousand characters and illuminations.

3

It is true that Mr. Lewis contemplates a reality adequate to the profound necessities of life today. But it is no less true that it is easier to try to recognize it or something like it or the possible beginnings of it than to achieve it on that scale. Thus, the field in poetry is as great as it is in anything else. Nothing illustrates this better and nothing illustrates the importance of poetry better than this possibility that within it there may yet be found a reality adequate to the profound necessities of life today or for that matter any day. Miss Moore's poem is an instance of method and is not an example beyond the scale intended by her. She may well say:

Que ce n'est pas grand merveille de voir que l'Ostruche digére le fer, veu que les poulles n'en font pas moins.

For she is not a proud spirit. It may be that proud spirits love only the lion or the elephant with its howdah. Miss

Moore, however, loves all animals, fierce or mild, ancient or modern. When she observes them she is transported into the presence of a recognizable reality, because, as it happens, she has the faculty of digesting the "harde yron" of appearance.

Effects of Analogy

I

THE SUPREME example of analogy in English is *Pilgrim's Progress*. This overwhelms us with direct analogy, that is to say: the personifications of allegory. Thus, in the Second Part where Christiana and young Mercy are on their way toward the Caelestial Country with Christiana's children to rejoin Christian, they come at evening to the house of the Interpreter. After the Interpreter has shown them his house he leads them into his garden and

as they were coming in from abroad, they espied a little robin with a great spider in his mouth. So they looked, and Mercy wondred; but Christiana said, what a disparagement is it to such a little pretty bird as the robin-red-breast is, he being also a bird above many that loveth to maintain a kind of sociableness with man; I had thought they had lived upon crums of bread, or upon other such harmless matter. I like him worse than I did.

The Interpreter then replied, This robin is an emblem very apt to set forth some professors by; for to sight they are as this robin, pretty of note colour and carriage. They seem also to have a very great love for professors that are sincere; and above all other to desire to sociate with, and to be in their company, as if they could live upon the good man's crums. They pretend also that therefore it is that they frequent the house of the godly, and the appointments of the Lord; but when they are by themselves, as the robin, they can catch and gobble up spiders, they can change their diet, drink iniquity, and swallow down sin like water.

In French, the supreme example of analogy is, probably, the *Fables* of La Fontaine. Of these, none is better known than the fable of "The Crow and the Fox," which goes, in the translation of Edward Marsh, as follows:

> *A Crow sat perched upon an oak,*
> *And in his beak he held a cheese.*
> *A fox snuffed up the savoury breeze,*
> *And thus in honey'd accent spoke:*
> *"O Prince of Crows, such grace of mien*
> *Has never in these parts been seen.*
> *If but your song be half as good,*
> *You are the Phoenix of the wood!"*
> *The Crow, beside himself with pleasure,*
> *And eager to display his voice,*
> *Opened his beak, and dropt his treasure.*
> *The Fox was on it in a trice.*
> *"Learn, sir," said he, "that flatterers live*
> *On those who swallow what they say.*
> *A cheese is not too much to give*
> *For such a piece of sound advice!"*
> *The Crow, ashamed t'have been such easy prey,*
> *Swore, though too late, he shouldn't catch him twice.*

As we read Bunyan we are distracted by the double
sense of the analogy and we are rather less engaged by
the symbols than we are by what is symbolized. The
other meaning divides our attention and this diminishes
our enjoyment of the story. But of such an indisputable
masterpiece it must be true that one reader, oblivious of
the other meaning, reads it for the story and another
reader, oblivious of the story, reads it for the other mean-
ing; and that each finds in perfection what he wants. But
there is a third reader, one for whom the story and the
other meaning should come together like two aspects that
combine to produce a third or, if they do not combine,
inter-act, so that one influences the other and produces
an effect similar in kind to the prismatic formations that
occur about us in nature in the case of reflections and re-
fractions. Bunyan nowhere produces these prismatic crys-
tallizations. As for such things, he might as well be a
collection of primitive woodcuts. In La Fontaine, there
is a difference. We are not distracted. Our attention is on
the symbol, which is interesting in itself. The other
meaning does not dog the symbol like its shadow. It is
not attached to it. Here the effect of analogy almost
ceases to exist and the reason for this is, of course, that
we are not particularly conscious of it. We do not have
to stand up to it and take it. It is like a play of thought,
some trophy that we ourselves gather, some meaning
that we ourselves supply. It is like a pleasant shadow,
faint and volatile. In Bunyan, it is the other meaning that
is the solid matter; in La Fontaine, the solid matter is

the story. The difference may be a national difference. We are interested in it only as a difference.

2

Commonly, analogy is a term in logic. Susan Stebbing in her *Logic in Practice* says:

Inference by analogy consists in inferring that, since two cases are alike in certain respects, they will also be alike in some other respect. For example, since Mars resembles the Earth in certain respects, we infer that Mars also is inhabited. This may be a very risky inference, for Mars differs from the Earth in some respects, and these differences may be relevant to the property of being inhabited.

Now, we are not thinking, here, of analogy in this narrow sense. We are thinking of it as likeness, as resemblance between parallels and yet parallels that are parallels only in the imagination, and we are thinking of it in its relation to poetry. Finally we are thinking of it from the point of view of the effect it produces. The other day, Kenneth Burke, in the course of a review of Rosemond Tuve's *Elizabethan and Metaphysical Imagery*, referred to the introduction of rhetoric into the analysis of imagery. He said that it gave a clear picture of the ways in which logic, rhetoric and poetic are interwoven

in contrast with the doctrines of those who would confine logic to science, rhetoric to propaganda or advertis-

*ing, and thus leave for poetic a few spontaneous sensa-
tions not much higher in the intellectual scale than the
twitchings of a decerebrated frog.*

The analogy between the spontaneous sensations of a
poet and the muscular twitchings of a decerebrated frog
communicated Mr. Burke's antipathy to the doctrines on
which he was commenting and was a way of charac-
terizing those doctrines as at once futile, ugly and ludi-
crous. His analogy had its source in a feeling of scorn
and took the form of an image that expressed his scorn.
In short, his image had its origin in an emotion, was
charged with that emotion and became the medium for
communicating it. Thus, it belongs to that large class of
images of emotional origin in which the nature of the
image is analogous to the nature of the emotion from
which it springs; and when one speaks of images, one
means analogies. If, then, an emotional image or, say,
an emotional analogy communicates the emotion that
generates it, its effect is to arouse the same emotion in
others. There is nothing of this in the sort of analogy that
we find in *Pilgrim's Progress*. The very scale and de-
liberateness of allegory are against it. To be sure, *Pil-
grim's Progress* is prose. In a long poem, so many emo-
tions, so many sensations, are stirred up into activity
that, after a time, the reader finds himself in a state of
such sensibility that it cannot be said that the scale and
deliberateness of allegory fail to produce an emotional
effect. A prolonged reading of Spenser's *Faerie Queene*,

for instance, creates just such a state of sensibility. In general, long poems have this attribute, derived from their very length, assuming that they have been charged throughout with the emotions of the poet.

In order to see how true it is that in images of emotional origin the image partakes of the nature of the emotion, let us analyze a passage from one of the poems of Allen Tate. He is looking at a young woman dead in her bed. He says:

> For look you how her body stiffly lies
> Just as she left it, unprepared to stay,
> The posture waiting on the sleeping eyes,
> While the body's life, deep as a covered well,
> Instinctive as the wind, busy as May,
> Burns out a secret passageway to hell.

He is moved by the ghastliness and ghostliness of the body before him. He communicates the ghastliness by a direct statement: her body stiffly lies. But the ghostliness he communicates by making of the posture one of death's attendants. The thoughts of life and death commingle. Under the hidden image of the tomb, her spirit is instinctive as the wind in its blind and fateful freedom.

A scene not too dissimilar gives rise to a different feeling in John Crowe Ransom. In his *Bells for John Whiteside's Daughter*, he begins by describing her quizzically and yet as a little old lady who used to harry the geese on her pond and, with a rod, make them rise:

But now go the bells, and we are ready,
In our house we are sternly stopped
To say we are vexed at her brown study,
Lying so primly propped.

What is it that Mr. Ransom feels at the sight of John Whiteside's daughter, dead, except the same quizzicality that he felt at the sight of her alive? He communicates this in a quizzical image of death as a brown study, but as a brown study vexing in the case of one that lies so primly propped. Neither Mr. Tate nor Mr. Ransom is an emotional poet. Nor with such men is it a question of degree. Rather, their sensibilities have large orbits.

We have not been dealing, up to this point, with the appositeness of figures of speech but with their emotional authenticity, which they have the power to propagate. The emotional analogy is only one. When St. Matthew in his Gospel says that Jesus went about all the cities, teaching and preaching, and that

when he saw the multitudes, he was moved with com-
passion on them, because they . . . were scattered
abroad, as sheep having no shepherd,

the analogy between the multitudes scattered abroad and sheep having no shepherd is not an emotional analogy. On the contrary, it is as if Matthew had poised himself if only for an instant, had invoked his imagination and had made a choice of what it offered to his mind, a choice based on the degree of the appositeness of the image. He could do this without being notably deliberate because the imagination does not require for its projections the same amount of time that the reason requires. I spoke a moment ago of a reader for whom the two elements of an analogy should combine to produce a third. There is still another reader for whom the effect of analogy is the effect of the degree of appositeness, for whom the imaginative projection, the imaginative deviation, raises the question of rightness, as if in the vast association of ideas there existed for every object its appointed objectification. In such a case, the object and its image become inseparable. It follows that for this fourth reader the effect of analogy is the effect of consummation. The example from Matthew is not only a good example, but a familiar one. One almost equally familiar is from the Greek Anthology, in Professor Mackail's translation:

Even as a vine on her dry pole I support myself now on a staff and death calls me to Hades.

This epigram has about it something of the modern sense of epigram. Leonidas does not compare himself to a vine on her dry pole without a certain slyness. The image is not only that of the old man wandering on the edge of night. It includes, also, something of his tatteredness, something of the weather-beaten figure of the vagabond, which by its eccentricity arouses the sense of pathos but not the feeling of sorrow. These two citations, the one of sheep having no shepherd and the other of the vine on her dry pole, quite adequately illustrate the discipline that comes from appositeness in the highest degree.

It is primarily a discipline of rightness. The poet is constantly concerned with two theories. One relates to the imagination as a power within him not so much to destroy reality at will as to put it to his own uses. He comes to feel that his imagination is not wholly his own but that it may be part of a much larger, much more potent imagination, which it is his affair to try to get at. For this reason, he pushes on and lives, or tries to live, as Paul Valéry did, on the verge of consciousness. This often results in poetry that is marginal, subliminal. The same theory exists in relation to prose, to painting and other arts. The second theory relates to the imagination as a power within him to have such insights into reality as will make it possible for him to be sufficient as a poet in the very center of consciousness. This results, or should result, in a central poetry. Dr. Whitehead concluded his *Modes of Thought* by saying:

> . . . the purpose of philosophy is to rationalize mysticism. . . . Philosophy is akin to poetry, and both of them seek to express that ultimate good sense which we term civilization.

The proponents of the first theory believe that it will be a part of their achievement to have created the poetry of the future. It may be that the poetry of the future will be to the poetry of the present what the poetry of the present is to the ballad. The proponents of the second theory believe that to create the poetry of the present is an incalculable difficulty, which rarely is achieved, fully and robustly, by anyone. They think that there is enough and more than enough to do with what faces us and concerns us directly and that in poetry as an art, and, for that matter, in any art, the central problem is always the problem of reality. The adherents of the imagination are mystics to begin with and pass from one mysticism to another. The adherents of the central are also mystics to begin with. But all their desire and all their ambition is to press away from mysticism toward that ultimate good sense which we term civilization. The analogy of Matthew and the image of Leonidas are particles of that ultimate good sense.

In departing from the finality and rightness of two ancient specimens, let us make use of a third for the purpose of pointing out that it is not possible to measure the distances away from rightness except in the roughest manner nor to indicate anything more than crude differences of effect. Virgil, in the first book of the *Georgics*, in Day Lewis' translation, says:

> *Winter's an off-time*
> *For farmers . . .*
> *   and they forget their worries;*
> *Just as, when ships in cargo have come to port at last,*
> *Glad to be home the sailors adorn their poops with garlands.*

This expresses an analogy between farmers after a summer and sailors after a voyage, fortified by secondary analogies between the worries of farmers and the trials of sailors, between crops and cargoes and between harvesting and making port. It is therefore a figure over which Virgil did something more than poise himself for an instant. It is a considered elaboration, a prototype of the considered elaborations with which in the eighteenth century, say, English poets were accustomed to embellish their pages. It does not click. If it is apposite at all it is only after we have thought about it and by that time we have lost interest in it. It is one of the multitude of figures of speech that are merely idle. It does not raise any question of taste. Nothing in Virgil could. One remembers the description of Virgil as the delight of all men of taste. Nevertheless, to go back to Allen Tate, it is just not a thing that

> . . . *strikes like a hawk the crouching hare.*

It would not be hard to find elsewhere examples of analogy displaying this or that defect, artificiality, incongruity, lack of definition. This is not an anatomy of metaphor. Nor is it an attempt to do more than to single out a few of the effects of analogy. The field must be one which has already been examined, for other purposes, by literary critics and historians, writers on aesthetics, psychologists, Freudians. Poetry is almost incredibly one of the effects of analogy. This statement involves much more than the analogy of figures of speech, since otherwise poetry would be little more than a trick. But it is almost incredibly the outcome of figures of speech or, what is the same thing, the outcome of the operation of one imagination on another through the instrumentality of the figures. To identify poetry and metaphor or metamorphosis is merely to abbreviate the last remark. There is always an analogy between nature and the imagination, and possibly poetry is merely the strange rhetoric of that parallel: a rhetoric in which the feeling of one man is communicated to another in words of the exquisite appositeness that takes away all their verbality.

3

Another mode of analogy is to be found in the personality of the poet. But this mode is no more limited to the poet than the mode of metaphor is so limited. This mode proposes for study the poet's sense of the world as the source of poetry. The corporeal world exists as the common denominator of the incorporeal worlds of its inhabitants. If there are people who live only in the corporeal world, enjoying the wind and the weather and supplying standards of normality, there are other people who are not so sure of the wind and the weather and who supply standards of abnormality. It is the poet's sense of the world that is the poet's world. The corporeal world, the familiar world of the commonplace, in short, our world, is one sense of the analogy that develops between our world and the world of the poet. The poet's sense of the world is the other sense. It is the analogy between these two senses that concerns us.

We could not speak of our world as something to be distinguished from the poet's sense of it unless we objectified it and recognized it as having an existence apart from the projection of his personality, as land and sea, sky and cloud. He himself desires to make the distinction as part of the process of realizing himself. Once the distinction has been made, it becomes an instrument for the exploration of poetry. By means of it we can determine the relation of the poet to his subject. This would be simple if he wrote about his own world. We could compare it with ours. But what he writes about is his sense of our world. If he is a melancholy person he gives us a melancholy sense of our world. By way of illustration, here is a passage from James Thomson's *The City of Dreadful Night*:

> We do not ask a longer term of strife,
>   Weakness and weariness and nameless woes:
> We do not claim renewed and endless life
>   When this which is our torment here shall close,
> An everlasting conscious inanition!
> We yearn for speedy death in full fruition,
>   Dateless oblivion and divine repose.

On the other hand, a stronger man, Walt Whitman, in *A Clear Midnight* gives us this:

> This is thy hour, O soul, thy free flight into the wordless,
> Away from books, away from art, the day erased, the
>   lesson done,
> Thee fully forth emerging, silent, gazing, pondering the
>   themes thou lovest best,
> Night, sleep, death and the stars.

The illustrations are endless but really none is required.

A man's sense of the world is born with him and persists, and penetrates the ameliorations of education and experience of life. His species is as fixed as his genus. For each man, then, certain subjects are congenital. Now, the poet manifests his personality, first of all, by his choice of subject. Temperament is a more explicit word than personality and would no doubt be the exact word to use, since it emphasizes the manner of thinking and feeling. It is agreeable to think of the poet as a whole biological mechanism and not as a subordinate mechanism within that larger one. Temperament, too, has attracted a pejorative meaning. It should be clear that in dealing with the choice of subject we are dealing with one of the vital factors in poetry or in any art. Great numbers of poets come and go who have never had a subject at all. What is true of poets in this respect is equally true of painters, as the existence of schools of painters all doing more or less the same thing at the same time demonstrates. The leader of the school has a subject. But his followers merely have his subject. Thus Picasso has a subject, a subject that devours him and devastates his region. Possibly a better illustration would be one that is less intimidating. Whether we like it or not, all of us who have radios or who go to the movies hear a great deal of popular music. Usually this is music without a subject. You have only to tabulate the titles of the songs you hear over a short period of time to convince yourself of this. The titles are trivial, catchy, trite and silly. Love is not a subject unless the writer of the song is in love. A man peddles love-songs because it is easier to do than it is to peddle coconuts, and this is as true of the man who writes the words as it is of the man who writes the music.

What is the poet's subject? It is his sense of the world. For him, it is inevitable and inexhaustible. If he departs from it he becomes artificial and laborious and while his artifice may be skillful and his labor perceptive no one knows better than he that what he is doing, under such circumstances, is not essential to him. It may help him to feel that it may be essential to someone else. But this justification, though it might justify what he does in the eyes of all the world, would never quite justify him in his own eyes. There is nothing of selfishness in this. It is often said of a man that his work is autobiographical in spite of every subterfuge. It cannot be otherwise. Certainly, from the point of view from which we are now regarding it, it cannot be otherwise, even though it may be totally without reference to himself. There was a time when the ivory tower was merely a place of seclusion, like a cottage on a hill-top or a cabin by the sea. Today, it is a kind of lock-up of which our intellectual constables are the appointed wardens. Is it not time that someone questioned this degradation, not for the purpose of restoring the isolation of the tower but in order to establish the integrity of its builder? Our rowdy gun-men may not appreciate what comes from that tower. Others do. Was there ever any poetry more wholly the poetry of the

ivory tower than the poetry of Mallarmé? Was there ever
any music more wholly the music of the ivory tower than
the music of Debussy?

The truth is that a man's sense of the world dictates
his subjects to him and that this sense is derived from his
personality, his temperament, over which he has little
control and possibly none, except superficially. It is not
a literary problem. It is the problem of his mind and
nerves. These sayings are another form of the saying
that poets are born not made. A poet writes of twilight
because he shrinks from noon-day. He writes about the
country because he dislikes the city, and he likes the one
and dislikes the other because of some trait of mind or
nerves; that is to say, because of something in himself
that influences his thinking and feeling. So seen, the
poet and his subject are inseparable. There are stresses
that he invites; there are stresses that he avoids. There
are colors that have the blandest effect on him; there are
others with which he can do nothing but find fault. In
music he likes the strings. But the horn shocks him. A
flat landscape extending in all directions to immense dis-
tances placates him. But he shrugs his shoulders at moun-
tains. One young woman seems to be someone that he
would like to know; another seems to be someone that he
must know without fail.

Recently, a very great deal has been said about the
relation of the poet to his community and to other people,
and as the propaganda on behalf of the community and
other people gathers momentum a great deal more will

be said. But if a poet's subject is congenital this is beside the point. Or is it? The ivory tower was offensive if the man who lived in it wrote, there, of himself for himself. It was not offensive if he used it because he could do nothing without concentration, as no one can, and because, there, he could most effectively struggle to get at his subject, even if his subject happened to be the community and other people, and nothing else. It may be that the poet's congenital subject is precisely the community and other people. If it is not, he may have to ask Shostakovich and Prokofiev and their fellow musicians and such writers as Michael Zoshchenko what to do next. These men, who backslide once in so often, should know. They are experienced.

The second way by which a poet manifests his personality is by his style. This is too well understood to permit discussion. What has just been said with respect to choice of subject applies equally to style. The individual dialect of a poet who happens to have one, analogous to the speech common to his time and place and yet not that common speech, is in the same position as the language of poetry generally when the language of poetry generally is not the common speech. Both produce effects singular to analogy. Beyond that the dialect is not in point.

A man's sense of the world may be only his own or it may be the sense of many people. Whatever it is it involves his fate. It may involve only his own or it may involve that of many people. The measure of the poet is the measure of his sense of the world and of the extent to which it involves the sense of other people. We have to stop and think now and then of what he writes as implicit with that significance. Thus in the lines of Leonidas:

Even as a vine on her dry pole I support myself now on a staff and death calls me to Hades

we have to think of the reality and to read the lines as one having the reality at heart: an old man at that point at which antiquity begins to resume what everything else has left behind; or if you think of the lines as a figuration of despair on the part of the poet, and it is possible to change them into such a figuration, to read them as lines communicating a feeling that it was not within the poet's power to suppress.

4

Still another mode of analogy is to be found in the music of poetry. It is a bit old hat and romantic and, no doubt at all, the dated forms are intolerable. In recent years, poetry began to change character about the time when painting began to change character. Each lost a certain euphrasy. But, after all, the music of poetry has not come to an end. Is not Eliot a musical poet? Listen to part of what the lamp hummed of the moon in *Rhapsody on a Windy Night*:

> *A washed-out smallpox cracks her face,*
> *Her hand twists a paper rose,*
> *That smells of dust and old Cologne,*
> *She is alone*

> With all the old nocturnal smells
> That cross and cross across her brain.
> The reminiscence comes
> Of sunless dry geraniums
> And dust in crevices,
> Smells of chestnuts in the streets
> And female smells in shuttered rooms
> And cigarettes in corridors
> And cocktail smells in bars.

This is a specimen of what is meant by music today. It contains rhymes at irregular intervals and it is intensely cadenced. But yesterday, or the day before, the time from which the use of the word "music" in relation to poetry has come down to us, music meant something else. It meant metrical poetry with regular rhyme schemes repeated stanza after stanza. All of the stanzas were alike in form. As a result of this, what with the repetitions of the beats of the lines, and the constant and recurring harmonious sounds, there actually was a music. But with the disappearance of all this, the use of the word "music" in relation to poetry is as I said a moment ago a bit old hat: anachronistic. Yet the passage from Eliot was musical. It is simply that there has been a change in the nature of what we mean by music. It is like the change from Haydn to a voice intoning. It is like the voice of an actor reciting or declaiming or of some other figure concealed, so that we cannot identify him, who speaks with a measured voice which is often disturbed by his feeling for what he says. There is no accompaniment. If occasionally the poet touches the triangle or one of the cymbals, he does it only because he feels like doing it. Instead of a musician we have an orator whose speech sometimes resembles music. We have an eloquence and it is that eloquence that we call music every day, without having much cause to think about it.

What has this music to do with analogy? When we hear the music of one of the great narrative musicians, as it tells its tale, it is like finding our way through the dark not by the aid of any sense but by an instinct that makes it possible for us to move quickly when the music moves quickly, slowly when the music moves slowly. It is a speed that carries us on and through every winding, once more to the world outside of the music at its conclusion. It affects our sight of what we see and leaves it ambiguous, somewhat like one thing, somewhat like another. In the meantime the tale is being told and the music excites us and we identify it with the story and it becomes the story and the speed with which we are following it. When it is over, we are aware that we have had an experience very much like the story just as if we had participated in what took place. It is exactly as if we had listened with complete sympathy to an emotional recital. The music was a communication of emotion. It would not have been different if it had been the music of poetry or the voice of the protagonist telling the tale or speaking out his sense of the world. How many things we should have found like in either case!

5

I have spoken of several kinds of analogy. I began with the personifications of Bunyan and the animalizations of La Fontaine. I then spoke of emotional images, taking illustrations from several sources, principally Kenneth Burke. Next I spoke of what may be called voluntary images, quoting from St. Matthew, Leonidas of Tarentum and Virgil. Finally I spoke of what may be called involuntary images, quoting from James Thomson and Walt Whitman and referring to music. It is time, therefore, to attempt a few generalizations, slight as the data may be. Accordingly, our first generalization is this: Every image is the elaboration of a particular of the subject of the image. If this is true it is a realistic explanation of the origin of images. Let us go back to the quotation from St. Matthew. Jesus went about all the cities, teaching and preaching, and

when he saw the multitudes, he was moved with compassion on them, because they . . . were scattered abroad, as sheep having no shepherd.

The analogy between men and sheep does not exist under all circumstances. There came into Matthew's mind in respect to Jesus going about, teaching and preaching, the thought that Jesus was a shepherd and immediately the multitudes scattered abroad and sheep having that particular in common became interchangeable. The image is an elaboration of the particular of the shepherd. In the lines from Leonidas:

Even as a vine on her dry pole I support myself now on a staff and death calls me to Hades

the particular is the staff. This becomes the dry pole, and the vine follows after. There is no analogy between a vine and an old man under all circumstances. But when one supports itself on a dry pole and the other on a staff, the case is different. Two casual illustrations are not enough to establish a principle. But they are enough to suggest the possibility of a principle.

Our second generalization, based on even slighter data, and proposed in the same experimental way, is this: Every image is a restatement of the subject of the image in the terms of an attitude. The metaphor from Kenneth Burke illustrates this. Since it has already been analyzed, I merely refer to it. If there is any merit to what was said about the sense of the world, that also illustrates the principle.

Our third generalization is this: Every image is an intervention on the part of the image-maker. One does not feel the need of so many reservations, if of any, in the case of this principle. But then of the three it is the one that matters least. It refers to the sense of the world, as the second principle did, and it could be said to be a phase of the second principle, if it did not refer to style in addition to the sense of the world. The second principle does not refer to style.

It is time, too, to attempt a few simplifications of the whole subject by way of summing it up and of coming to an end. With one or two exceptions, all of the examples that we have made use of have been pictorial. The image has been descriptive or explanatory of the subject of the image. To say the same thing another way, the thing stated has been accompanied by a restatement and the restatement has illustrated and given definition to the thing stated. The thing stated and the restatement have constituted an analogy. The venerable, the fundamental books of the human spirit are vast collections of such analogies and it is the analogies that have helped to make these books what they are. The pictorializations of poetry include much more than figures of speech. We have not been studying images, but, however crudely, analogies, of which images are merely a part. Analogies are much the larger subject. And analogies are elusive. Take the case of a man for whom reality is enough, as, at the end of his life, he returns to it like a man returning from Nowhere to his village and to everything there that is tangible and visible, which he has come to cherish and wants to be near. He sees without images. But is he not seeing a clarified reality of his own? Does he not dwell in an analogy? His imageless world is, after all, of the same sort as a world full of the obvious analogies of happiness or unhappiness, innocence or tragedy, thoughtlessness or the heaviness of the mind. In any case, these are the pictorializations of men, for whom the world exists as a world and for whom life exists as life, the objects of their passions, the objects before which they come and speak, with intense choosing, words that we remember and make our own. Their words have made a world that transcends the world and a life livable in that transcendence. It is a transcendence achieved by means of the minor effects of figurations and the major effects of the poet's sense of the world and of the motive music of his poems and it is the imaginative dynamism of all these analogies together. Thus poetry becomes and is a transcendent analogue composed of the particulars of reality, created by the poet's sense of the world, that is to say, his attitude, as he intervenes and interposes the appearances of that sense.

Imagination as Value

L‍T DOES not seem possible to say of the imagination that it has a certain single characteristic which of itself gives it a certain single value as, for example, good or evil. To say such a thing would be the same thing as to say that the reason is good or evil or, for that matter, that human nature is good or evil. Since that is my first point, let us discuss it.

Pascal called the imagination the mistress of the world. But as he seems never to have spoken well of it, it is certain that he did not use this phrase to speak well of it. He called it the deceptive element in man, the mistress of error and duplicity and yet not always that, since there would be an infallible measure of truth if there were an infallible measure of untruth. But being most often false, it gives no sign of its quality and indicates in the same way both the true and the false. A little farther on in his *Pensées* he speaks of magistrates, their red robes, their ermines in which they swathe themselves, like furry cats, the palaces in which they sit in judgment, the fleurs-de-lis, and the whole necessary, august apparatus. He says, and he enjoys his own malice in saying it, that if medical men did not have their cassocks and the mules they wore and if doctors did not have their square hats and robes four times too large, they would never have been able to dupe the world, which is incapable of resisting so genuine a display. He refers to soldiers and kings, of whom he speaks with complete caution and respect, saying that they establish themselves by force, the others "par grimace." He justifies monarchs by the strength they possess and says that it is necessary to have a well-defined reason to regard like anyone else the Grand Seigneur surrounded, in his superb seraglio, by forty thousand janissaries.

However this may be, if respect for magistrates can be established by their robes and ermines and if justice can be made to prevail by the appearance of the seats of justice and if vast populations can be brought to live peacefully in their homes and to lie down at night with a sense of security and to get up in the morning confident that the great machine of organized society is ready to carry them on, merely by dressing a few men in uniform and sending them out to patrol the streets, the sort of thing that was the object of Pascal's ridicule and that was, to his way of thinking, an evil, or something of an evil, becomes to our way of thinking a potent good. The truth is, of course, that we do not really control vast populations in this way. Pascal knew perfectly well that the chancellor had force behind him. If he felt in his day that medicine was an imaginary science, he would not feel so today. After all, Pascal's understanding of the imagination was a part of his understanding of everything else. As he lay dying, he experienced a violent convulsion. His sister, who attended him, described the scene. He had repeatedly asked that he might receive communion. His sister wrote:

> *God, who wished to reward a desire so fervent and so just, suspended this convulsion as by a miracle and restored his judgment completely as in the perfection of his health, in a manner that the parish priest, entering into his room with the sacrament, cried to him: "Here is he whom you have so much desired." These words completely roused him and as the priest approached to give him communion, he made an effort, he raised himself half way without help to receive it with more respect; and the priest having interrogated him, following the custom, on the principal mysteries of the faith, he responded distinctly: "Yes, monsieur, I believe all that with all my heart." Then he received the sacred wafer and extreme unction with feelings so tender that he poured out tears. He replied to everything, thanked the priest and as the priest blessed him with the holy ciborium, he said, "Let God never forsake me."*

Thus, in the very act of dying, he clung to what he himself had called the delusive faculty. When I said a moment ago that he had never spoken well of it, I did not overlook the fact that "this superb power, the enemy of reason," to use his own words, did not, and could not, always seem the same to him. In a moment of indifference, he said that the imagination disposes all things and that it is the imagination that creates beauty, justice and happiness. In these various ways, the example of Pascal demonstrates how the good of the imagination may be evil and its evil good. The imagination is the power of the mind over the possibilities of things; but if this constitutes a certain single characteristic, it is the source not of a certain single value but of as many values as reside in the possibilities of things.

A second difficulty about value is the difference between the imagination as metaphysics and as a power of the mind over external objects, that is to say, reality. Ernst Cassirer in his *An Essay on Man* says:

> *In romantic thought the theory of poetic imagination had reached its climax. Imagination is no longer that special human activity which builds up the human world of art. It now has universal metaphysical value. Poetic imagination is the only clue to reality. Fichte's idealism is based upon his conception of "productive imagination." Schelling declared in his* System of Transcendental Idealism *that art is the consummation of philosophy. In nature, in morality, in history we are still living in the propylaeum of philosophical wisdom; in art we enter into the sanctuary itself. The true poem is not the work of the individual artist; it is the universe itself, the one work of art which is forever perfecting itself.*

Professor Cassirer speaks of this as "exuberant and ecstatic praise of poetic imagination." In addition, it is the language of what he calls "romantic thought" and by romantic thought he means metaphysics. When I speak of the power of the mind over external objects I have in mind, as external objects, works of art as, for example, the sculptures of Michelangelo with what Walter Pater calls "their wonderful strength verging, as in the things of the imagination great strength always does, on what is singular or strange," or, in architecture, the formidable public buildings of the British or the architecture and decoration of churches, as, say, in the case of the Jesuit church at Lucerne, where one might so easily pass from the real to the visionary without consciousness of change. Imagination, as metaphysics, leads us in one direction and, as art, in another.

When we consider the imagination as metaphysics, we realize that it is in the nature of the imagination itself that we should be quick to accept it as the only clue to reality. But alas! we are no sooner so disposed than we encounter the logical positivists. In *Language, Truth and Logic*, Professor Ayer says that

it is fashionable to speak of the metaphysician as a kind of misplaced poet. As his statements have no literal meaning, they are not subject to any criteria of truth or falsehood; but they may still seem to express, or arouse, emotions, and thus be subject to ethical or aesthetic standards. And it is suggested that they may have considerable value, as means of moral inspiration, or even as works of art. In this way, an attempt is made to compensate the metaphysician for his extrusion from philosophy.

It appears from this that the imagination as metaphysics, from the point of view of the logical positivist, has at least seeming values. During the last few months, the *New Statesman* of London has been publishing letters growing out of a letter sent to it by a visitor to Oxford, who reported that Professor Ayer's book had "acquired almost the status of a philosophic Bible." This led Professor Joad to look up the book and see for himself. He reported that the book teaches that

> *If . . . God is a metaphysical term, if, that is to say, He belongs to a reality which transcends the world of sense-experience . . . to say that He exists is neither true nor false. This position . . . is neither atheist nor agnostic; it cuts deeper than either, by asserting that all talk about God, whether pro or anti, is twaddle.*

What is true of one metaphysical term is true of all.

Then, too, before going on, we must somehow cleanse the imagination of the romantic. We feel, without being particularly intelligent about it, that the imagination as metaphysics will survive logical positivism unscathed. At the same time, we feel, and with the sharpest possible intelligence, that it is not worthy to survive if it is to be identified with the romantic. The imagination is one of the great human powers. The romantic belittles it. The imagination is the liberty of the mind. The romantic is a failure to make use of that liberty. It is to the imagination what sentimentality is to feeling. It is a failure of the imagination precisely as sentimentality is a failure of feeling. The imagination is the only genius. It is intrepid and eager and the extreme of its achievement lies in abstraction. The achievement of the romantic, on the contrary, lies in minor wish-fulfillments and it is incapable of abstraction. In any case and without continuing to contrast the two things, one wants to elicit a sense of the imagination as something vital. In that sense one must deal with it as metaphysics.

If we escape destruction at the hands of the logical positivists and if we cleanse the imagination of the taint of the romantic, we still face Freud. What would he have said of the imagination as the clue to reality and of a culture based on the imagination? Before jumping to the conclusion that at last there is no escape, is it not possible that he might have said that in a civilization based on science there could be a science of illusions? He does in fact say that "So long as a man's early years are influenced by the religious thought-inhibition . . . as well as by the sexual one, we cannot really say what he is actually like." If when the primacy of the intelligence has been achieved, one can really say what a man is actually like, what could be more natural than a science of illusions? Moreover, if the imagination is not quite the clue to reality now, might it not become so then? As for the present, what have we, if we do not have science, except the imagination? And who is to say of its deliberate fictions arising out of the contemporary mind that they are not the forerunners of some such science? There is more than the romantic in the statement that the true work of art, whatever it may be, is not the work of the individual artist. It is time and it is place, as these perfect themselves.

To regard the imagination as metaphysics is to think of it as part of life, and to think of it as part of life is to realize the extent of artifice. We live in the mind. One way of demonstrating what it means to live in the mind is to imagine a discussion of the world between two people born blind, able to describe their images, so far as they have images, without the use of images derived from other people. It would not be our world that would be discussed. Still another illustration may help. A man in Paris does not imagine the same sort of thing that a native of Uganda imagines. If each could transmit his imagination to the other, so that the man in Paris, lying awake at night, could suddenly hear a footfall that meant the presence of some inimical and merciless monstrosity, and if the man in Uganda found himself in, say, the Muenster at Basel and experienced what is to be experienced there, what words would the Parisian find to forestall his fate and what understanding would the Ugandan have of his incredible delirium? If we live in the mind, we live with the imagination. It is a commonplace to realize the extent of artifice in the external world and to say that Florence is more imaginative than Dublin, that blue and white Munich is more imaginative than white and green Havana, and so on; or to say that, in this town, no single public object of the imagination exists, while in the Vatican City, say, no public object exists that is not an object of the imagination. What is engaging us at the moment has nothing to do with the external world. We are concerned with the extent of artifice within us and, almost parenthetically, with the question of its value.

What, then, is it to live in the mind with the imagination, yet not too near to the fountains of its rhetoric, so that one does not have a consciousness only of grandeurs, of incessant departures from the idiom and of inherent altitudes? Only the reason stands between it and the reality for which the two are engaged in a struggle. We have no particular interest in this struggle because we know that it will continue to go on and that there will never be an outcome. We lose sight of it until Pascal, or someone else, reminds us of it. We say that it is merely a routine and the more we think about it the less able we are to see that it has any heroic aspects or that the spirit is at stake or that it may involve the loss of the world. Is there in fact any struggle at all and is the idea of one merely a bit of academic junk? Do not the two carry on together in the mind like two brothers or two sisters or even like young Darby and young Joan? Darby says, "It is often true that what is most rational appears to be most imaginative, as in the case of Picasso." Joan replies, "It is often true, also, that what is most imaginative appears to be most rational, as in the case of Joyce. Life is hard and dear and it is the hardness that makes it dear." And Darby says, "Speaking of Joyce and the co-existence of opposites, do you remember the story that Joyce tells of

Pascal in *Portrait of the Artist as a Young Man?* Stephen
said:

> —*Pascal, if I remember rightly, would not suffer his*
> *mother to kiss him as he feared the contact of her sex—*
> —*Pascal was a pig—said Cranby.*
> —*Aloysius Gonzaga, I think, was of the same mind—*
> *Stephen said.*
> —*And he was another pig then—said Cranby.*
> —*The church calls him a saint—Stephen objected."*

How is it that we should be speaking of the prize of
the spirit and of the loss, or gain, of the world, in con-
nection with the relations between reason and the imagi-
nation? It may be historically true that the reason of a
few men has always been the reason of the world. Not-
withstanding this, we live today in a time dominated
by great masses of men and, while the reason of a few
men may underlie what they do, they act as their imagi-
nations impel them to act. The world may, certainly, be
lost to the poet but it is not lost to the imagination. I
speak of the poet because we think of him as the orator
of the imagination. And I say that the world is lost to
him, certainly, because, for one thing, the great poems
of heaven and hell have been written and the great poem
of the earth remains to be written. I suppose it is that
poem that will constitute the true prize of the spirit and
that until it is written many lesser things will be so re-
garded, including conquests that are not unimaginable.
One wants to consider the imagination on its most mo-

mentous scale. Today this scale is not the scale of poetry, nor of any form of literature or art. It is the scale of international politics and in particular of communism. Communism is not the measure of humanity. But I limit myself to an allusion to it as a phenomenon of the imagination. Surely the diffusion of communism exhibits imagination on its most momentous scale. This is because whether or not communism is the measure of humanity, the words themselves echo back to us that it has for the present taken the measure of an important part of humanity. With the collapse of other beliefs, this grubby faith promises a practicable earthly paradise. The only earthly paradise that even the best of other faiths has been able to promise has been one in man's noblest image and this has always required an imagination that has not yet been included in the fortunes of mankind.

The difference between an imagination that is engaged by the materialism of communism and one that is engaged by the projects of idealism is a difference in nature. It is not that the imagination is versatile but that there are different imaginations. The commonest idea of an imaginative object is something large. But apparently with the Japanese it is the other way round and with them the commonest idea of an imaginative object is something small. With the Hindu it appears to be something vermicular, with the Chinese, something round and with the Dutch, something square. If these evidences do not establish the point, it can hardly be because the point needs establishing. A comparison between the Bible and poetry is relevant. It cannot be said that the Bible, the most widely distributed book in the world, is the poorest. Nor can it be said that it owes its distribution to the poetry it contains. If poetry should address itself to the same needs and aspirations, the same hopes and fears, to which the Bible addresses itself, it might rival it in distribution. Poetry does not address itself to beliefs. Nor could it ever invent an ancient world full of figures that had been known and become endeared to its readers for centuries. Consequently, when critics of poetry call upon it to do some of the things that the Bible does, they overlook the certainty that the Biblical imagination is one thing and the poetic imagination, inevitably, something else. We cannot look at the past or the future except by means of the imagination but again the imagination of backward glances is one thing and the imagination of looks ahead something else. Even the psychologists concede this present particular, for, with them, memory involves a reproductive power, and looks ahead involve a creative power: the power of our expectations. When we speak of the life of the imagination, we do not mean man's life as it is affected by his imagination but the life of the faculty itself. Accordingly, when we think of the permeation of man's life by the imagination, we must not think of it as a life permeated by a single thing but by a class of things. We use our imagination with respect to every man of whom we take notice when by a glance we make up our mind about him. The differences so defined entail differences of value. The imagination that is satisfied by politics, whatever the nature of the politics, has not the same value as the imagination that seeks to satisfy, say, the universal mind, which, in the case of a poet, would be the imagination that tries to penetrate to basic images, basic emotions, and so to compose a fundamental poetry even older than the ancient world. Perhaps one drifts off into rhetoric here, but then there is nothing more congenial than that to the imagination.

Of imaginative life as social form, let me distinguish at once between everyday living and the activity of cultural organization. A theater is a social form but it is also a cultural organization and it is not my purpose to discuss the imagination as an institution. Having in mind the extent to which the imagination pervades life, it seems curious that it does not pervade, or even create, social form more widely. It is an activity like seeing things or hearing things or any other sensory activity. Perhaps, if one collected instances of imaginative life as social form over a period of time, one might amass a prodigious number from among the customs of our lives. Our social attitudes, social distinctions and the insignia of social distinctions are instances. A ceremonious baptism, a ceremonious wedding, a ceremonious funeral are instances. It takes very little, however, to make a social form arising from the imagination stand out from the normal, and the fact that a form is abnormal is an argument for its suppression. Normal people do not accept something abnormal because it has its origin in an abnormal force like the imagination nor at all until they have somehow normalized it as by familiarity. Costume is an instance of imaginative life as social form. At the same time it is an instance of the acceptance of something incessantly abnormal by reducing it to the normal. It cannot be said that life as we live it from day to day wears an imaginative aspect. On the other hand, it can be said that the aspect of life as we live it from day to day conceals the imagination as social form. No one doubts that the forms of daily living secrete within themselves an infinite variety of things intelligible only to anthropologists nor that lives, like our own, lived after an incalculable number of preceding lives and in the accumulation of what they have left behind are socially complicated even when they appear to be socially innocent. To me, the accumulation of lives at a university has seemed to be a subject that might disclose something extraordinary. What is the residual effect of the years we spend at a university, the years of imaginative life, if ever in our lives there are such years, on the social form of our own future and on the social form of the future of the world of which we are part, when compared with the effects of our later economic and political years?

The discussion of the imagination as metaphysics has led us off a little to one side. This is justified, however, by the considerations, first, that the operation of the imagination in life is more significant than its operation in or in relation to works of art or perhaps I should have said, from the beginning, in arts and letters; second, that the imagination penetrates life; and finally, that its value

as metaphysics is not the same as its value in arts and
letters. In spite of the prevalence of the imagination in
life, it is probably true that the discussion of it in that
relation is incomparably less frequent and less intelligent
than the discussion of it in relation to arts and letters.
The constant discussion of imagination and reality is
largely a discussion not for the purposes of life but for the
purposes of arts and letters. I suppose that the reason for
this is that few people would turn to the imagination,
knowingly, in life, while few people would turn to any-
thing else, knowingly, in arts and letters. In life what is
important is the truth as it is, while in arts and letters
what is important is the truth as we see it. There is a
real difference here even though people turn to the im-
agination without knowing it in life and to reality with-
out knowing it in arts and letters. There are other pos-
sible variations of that theme but the theme itself is there.
Again in life the function of the imagination is so varied
that it is not well-defined as it is in arts and letters.
In life one hesitates when one speaks of the value of the
imagination. Its value in arts and letters is aesthetic.
Most men's lives are thrust upon them. The existence of
aesthetic value in lives that are forced on those that live
them is an improbable sort of thing. There can be lives,
nevertheless, which exist by the deliberate choice of
those that live them. To use a single illustration: it may
be assumed that the life of Professor Santayana is a life
in which the function of the imagination has had a func-
tion similar to its function in any deliberate work of art

or letters. We have only to think of this present phase of it, in which, in his old age, he dwells in the head of the world, in the company of devoted women, in their convent, and in the company of familiar saints, whose presence does so much to make any convent an appropriate refuge for a generous and human philosopher. To repeat, there can be lives in which the value of the imagination is the same as its value in arts and letters and I exclude from consideration as part of that statement any thought of poverty or wealth, being a *bauer* or being a king, and so on, as irrelevant.

The values of which it is common to think in relation to life are ethical values or moral values. The Victorians thought of these values in relation to arts and letters. It may be that the Russians mean to do about as the Victorians did, that is to say, think of the values of life in relation to arts and letters. A social value is simply an ethical value expressed by a member of the party. Between the wars, we lived, it may be said, in an era when some attempt was made to apply the value of arts and letters to life. These excursions of values beyond their spheres are part of a process which it is unnecessary to delineate. They are like the weather. We suffer from it and enjoy it and never quite know the one feeling from the other. It may, also, be altogether wrong to speak of the excursions of values beyond their spheres, since the question of the existence of spheres and the question of what is appropriate to them are not settled. Thus, something said the other day, that "An objective theory of value is needed in philosophy which does not depend upon unanalysable intuitions but relates goodness, truth and beauty to human needs in society," has a provocative sound. It is so easy for the poet to say that a learned man must go on being a learned man but that a poet respects no knowledge except his own and, again, that the poet does not yield to the priest. What the poet has in mind, when he says things of this sort, is that poetic value is an intrinsic value. It is not the value of knowledge. It is not the value of faith. It is the value of the imagination. The poet tries to exemplify it, in part, as I have tried to exemplify it here, by identifying it with an imaginative activity that diffuses itself throughout our lives. I say exemplify and not justify, because poetic value is an intuitional value and because intuitional values cannot be justified. We cannot very well speak of spheres of value and the transmission of a value, commonly considered appropriate to one sphere, to another, and allude to the peculiarity of roles, as the poet's role, without reminding ourselves that we are speaking of a thing in continual flux. There is no field in which this is more apparent than painting. Again, there is no field in which it is more constantly and more intelligently the subject of discussion than painting. The permissible reality in painting wavers with an insistence which is itself a value. One might just as well say the permissible imagination. It is as if the painter carried on with himself a continual argument as to whether what delights us in the exercise of the mind is what we produce or whether it is the exercise of a power of the mind.

A generation ago we should have said that the imagination is an aspect of the conflict between man and nature. Today we are more likely to say that it is an aspect of the conflict between man and organized society. It is part of our security. It enables us to live our own lives. We have it because we do not have enough without it. This may not be true as to each one of us, for certainly there are those for whom reality and the reason are enough. It is true of us as a race. A single, strong imagination is like a single, strong reason in this, that the extreme good of each is a spiritual good. It is not possible to say, as between the two, which is paramount. For that matter it is not always possible to say that they are two. When does a building stop being a product of the reason and become a product of the imagination? If we raise a building to an imaginative height, then the building becomes an imaginative building since height in itself is imaginative. It is the moderator of life as metempsychosis was of death. Nietzsche walked in the Alps in the caresses of reality. We ourselves crawl out of our offices and classrooms and become alert at the opera. Or we sit listening to music as in an imagination in which we believe. If the imagination is the faculty by which we import the unreal into what is real, its value is the value of the way of thinking by which we project the idea of God into the idea of man. It creates images that are independent of their originals since nothing is more certain than that the imagination is agreeable to the imagination. When one's aunt in California writes that the geraniums are up to her second-story window, we soon have them running over the roof. All this diversity, which I have intentionally piled up in confusion in this paragraph, is typical of the imagination. It may suggest that the imagination is the ignorance of the mind. Yet the imagination changes as the mind changes. I know an Italian who was a shepherd in Italy as a boy. He described his day's work. He said that at evening he was so tired he would lie down under a tree like a dog. This image was, of course, an image of his own dog. It was easy for him to say how tired he was by using the image of his tired dog. But given another mind, given the mind of a man of strong powers, accustomed to thought, accustomed to the essays of the imagination, and the whole imaginative substance changes. It is as if one could say that the imagination lives as the mind lives. The primitivism disappears. The Platonic resolution of diversity appears. The world is no longer an extraneous object, full of other extraneous objects, but an image. In the last analysis, it is with this image of the world that we are vitally concerned. We should not say, however, that the chief object of the imagination is to produce such an image. Among so many objects, it would be the merest improvisation to say of one, even though it is one with which we are vitally concerned, that it is the chief. The next step would be to assert that a particular image was the chief image. Again, it

would be the merest improvisation to say of any image of
the world, even though it was an image with which a vast
accumulation of imaginations had been content, that it
was the chief image. The imagination itself would not
remain content with it nor allow us to do so. It is the ir-
repressible revolutionist.

In spite of the confusion of values and the diversity of
aspects, one arrives eventually face to face with arts and
letters. I could take advantage of the pictures from the
Kaiser Friedrich Museum in Berlin, which are being
exhibited throughout the country and which many of
you, no doubt, have seen. The pictures by Poussin are
not the most marvelous pictures in this collection. Yet,
considered as objects of the imagination, how completely
they validate Gide's: "We must approach Poussin little
by little" and how firmly they sustain the statement made
a few moments ago that the imagination is the only
genius. There is also among these pictures a Giorgione,
the portrait of a young man, head and shoulders, in a
blue-purple blouse, or if not blue-purple, then a blue of
extraordinary enhancings. Vasari said of Giorgione that
he painted nothing that he had not seen in nature. This
portrait is an instance of a real object that is at the same
time an imaginative object. It has about it an imaginative
bigness of diction. We know that in poetry bigness and
gaiety are precious characteristics of the diction. This
portrait transfers that principle to painting. The subject
is severe but its embellishment, though no less severe, is
big and gay and one feels in the presence of this work that

one is also in the presence of an abundant and joyous spirit, instantly perceptible in what may be called the diction of the portrait. I could also take advantage, so far as letters are concerned, of a few first books of poems or a few first novels. One turns to first works of the imagination with the same expectation with which one turns to last works of the reason. But I am afraid that although one is, at last, face to face with arts and letters and, therefore, in the presence of particulars beyond particularization, it is prudent to limit discussion to a single point.

My final point, then, is that the imagination is the power that enables us to perceive the normal in the abnormal, the opposite of chaos in chaos. It does this every day in arts and letters. This may seem to be a merely capricious statement; for ordinarily we regard the imagination as abnormal per se. That point of view was approached in the reference to the academic struggle between reason and the imagination and again in the reference to the relation between the imagination and social form. The disposition toward a point of view derogatory to the imagination is an aversion to the abnormal. We see it in the common attitude toward modern arts and letters. The exploits of Rimbaud in poetry, if Rimbaud can any longer be called modern, and of Kafka in prose are deliberate exploits of the abnormal. It is natural for us to identify the imagination with those that extend its abnormality. It is like identifying liberty with those that abuse it. A literature overfull of abnormality and, certainly, present-day European literature, as one knows it, seems to be a literature full of abnormality, gives the reason an appearance of normality to which it is not, solely, entitled. The truth seems to be that we live in concepts of the imagination before the reason has established them. If this is true, then reason is simply the methodizer of the imagination. It may be that the imagination is a miracle of logic and that its exquisite divinations are calculations beyond analysis, as the conclusions of the reason are calculations wholly within analysis. If so, one understands perfectly the remark that "in the service of love and imagination nothing can be too lavish, too sublime or too festive." In the statement that we live in concepts of the imagination before the reason has established them, the word "concepts" means concepts of normality. Further, the statement that the imagination is the power that enables us to perceive the normal in the abnormal is a form of repetition of this statement. One statement does not demonstrate the other. The two statements together imply that the instantaneous disclosures of living are disclosures of the normal. This will seem absurd to those that insist on the solitude and misery and terror of the world. They will ask of what value is the imagination to them; and if their experience is to be considered, how is it possible to deny that they live in an imagination of evil? Is evil normal or abnormal? And how do the exquisite divinations of the poets and for that matter even the "aureoles of the saints" help them? But when we speak of perceiving the normal we have in mind the instinctive integrations which are the reason for living. Of what value is anything to the solitary and those that live in misery and terror, except the imagination?

Jean Paulhan, a Frenchman and a writer, is a man of great sense. He is a native of the region of Tarbes. Tarbes is a town in southwestern France in the High Pyrenees. Marshal Foch was born there. An equestrian statue of the Marshal stands there, high in the air, on a pedestal. In his *Les Fleurs de Tarbes*, Jean Paulhan says:

> *One sees at the entrance of the public garden of Tarbes, this sign:*
>
> > *It is forbidden*
> > *To enter into the garden*
> > *Carrying flowers.*

He goes on to say:

> *One finds it, also, in our time at the portal of literature. Nevertheless, it would be agreeable to see the girls of Tarbes (and the young writers) carrying a rose, a red poppy, an armful of red poppies.*

I repeat that Jean Paulhan is a man of great sense. But to be able to see the portal of literature, that is to say: the portal of the imagination, as a scene of normal love and normal beauty is, of itself, a feat of great imagination. It is the vista a man sees, seated in the public garden

of his native town, near by some effigy of a figure cele-
brated in the normal world, as he considers that the chief
problems of any artist, as of any man, are the problems
of the normal and that he needs, in order to solve them,
everything that the imagination has to give.

The Relations

between Poetry and Painting

I

ROGER FRY concluded a note on Claude by saying that "few of us live so strenuously as never to feel a sense of nostalgia for that Saturnian reign to which Virgil and Claude can waft us." He spoke in that same note of Corot and Whistler and Chinese landscape and certainly he might just as well have spoken, in relation to Claude, of many poets, as, for example, Chénier or Wordsworth. This is simply the analogy between two different forms of poetry. It might be better to say that it is the identity of poetry revealed as between poetry in words and poetry in paint.

Poetry, however, is not limited to Virgilian landscape, nor painting to Claude. We find the poetry of mankind in the figures of the old men of Shakespeare, say, and the old men of Rembrandt; or in the figures of Biblical women, on the one hand, and of the madonnas of all Europe, on the other; and it is easy to wonder whether the poetry of children has not been created by the poetry of the Child, until one stops to think how much of the poetry of the whole world is the poetry of children, both as they are and as they have been written of and painted, as if they were the creatures of a dimension in which life and poetry are one. The poetry of humanity is, of course, to be found everywhere.

There is a universal poetry that is reflected in everything. This remark approaches the idea of Baudelaire that there exists an unascertained and fundamental aesthetic, or order, of which poetry and painting are manifestations, but of which, for that matter, sculpture or music or any other aesthetic realization would equally be a manifestation. Generalizations as expansive as these: that there is a universal poetry that is reflected in everything or that there may be a fundamental aesthetic of which poetry and painting are related but dissimilar manifestations, are speculative. One is better satisfied by particulars.

No poet can have failed to recognize how often a detail, a propos or remark, in respect to painting, applies also to poetry. The truth is that there seems to exist a corpus of remarks in respect to painting, most often the remarks of painters themselves, which are as significant to poets as to painters. All of these details, to the extent that they have meaning for poets as well as for painters, are specific instances of relations between poetry and painting. I suppose, therefore, that it would be possible to study poetry by studying painting or that one could become a painter after one had become a poet, not to speak of carrying on in both métiers at once, with the economy of genius, as Blake did. Let me illustrate this point of the double value (and one might well call it the multifold value) of sayings for painters that mean as much for poets because they are, after all, sayings about art.

Does not the saying of Picasso that a picture is a horde of destructions also say that a poem is a horde of destructions? When Braque says "The senses deform, the mind forms," he is speaking to poet, painter, musician and sculptor. Just as poets can be affected by the sayings of painters, so can painters be affected by the sayings of poets and so can both be affected by sayings addressed to neither. For many examples, see Miss Sitwell's *Poet's Note-Book*. These details come together so subtly and so minutely that the existence of relations is lost sight of. This, in turn, dissipates the idea of their existence.

2

We may regard the subject, then, from two points of view, the first from the point of view of the man whose center is painting, whether or not he is a painter, the second from the point of view of the man whose center is poetry, whether or not he is a poet. To make use of the point of view of the man whose center is painting let me refer to the chapter in Leo Stein's *Appreciation* entitled "On Reading Poetry and Seeing Pictures." He says that, when he was a child, he became aware of composition in nature and gradually realized that art and composition are one. He began to experiment as follows:

I put on the table . . . an earthenware plate . . . and this I looked at every day for minutes or for hours. I had in mind to see it as a picture, and waited for it to become one. In time it did. The change came suddenly

*when the plate as an inventorial object . . . a certain
shape, certain colors applied to it . . . went over into
a composition to which all these elements were merely
contributory. The painted composition on the plate ceased
to be on it but became a part of a larger composition
which was the plate as a whole. I had made a beginning
to seeing pictorially.*

*What had been begun was carried out in all directions.
I wanted to be able to see anything as a composition and
found that it was possible to do this.*

He improvised a definition of art: that it is nature seen
in the light of its significance, and recognizing that this
significance was one of forms he added "formal" to "sig-
nificance."

Turning to education in hearing, he observed that
there is nothing comparable to the practice in composi-
tion that the visible world offers. By composition he
meant the compositional use of words: the use of their
existential meanings. Composition was his passion. He
considered that a formally complete picture is one in
which all the parts are so related to one another that they
all imply each other. Finally he said, "an excellent il-
lustration is the line from Wordsworth's Michael . . .
'And never lifted up a single stone.' " One might say of
a lazy workman, "He's been out there, just loafing, for
an hour and never lifted up a single stone," and no one
would think this great poetry. . . . These lines would
have no existential value; they would simply call atten-

tion to the lazy workman. But the compositional use by Wordsworth of his line makes it something entirely different. These simple words become weighted with the tragedy of the old shepherd, and are saturated with poetry. Their referential importance is slight, for the importance of the action to which they refer is not in the action itself, but in the meaning; and that meaning is borne by the words. Therefore this is a line of great poetry.

The selection of composition as a common denominator of poetry and painting is the selection of a technical characteristic by a man whose center was painting, even granting that he was not a man whom one thinks of as a technician. Poetry and painting alike create through composition.

Now, a poet looking for an analogy between poetry and painting and trying to take the point of view of a man whose center is poetry begins with a sense that the technical pervades painting to such a degree that the two are identified. This is untrue, since, if painting was purely technical, that conception of it would exclude the artist as a person. I want to say something, therefore, based on the sensibility of the poet and of the painter. I am not quite sure that I know what is meant by sensibility. I suppose that it means feeling or, as we say, the feelings. I know what is meant by nervous sensibility, as, when at a concert, the auditors, having composed themselves and resting there attentively, hear suddenly an outburst on the trumpets from which they shrink by way of a nervous reaction. The satisfaction that we have when we look out and find that it is a fine day or when we are looking at one of the limpid vistas of Corot in the pays de Corot seems to be something else. It is commonly said that the origins of poetry are to be found in the sensibility. We began with the conjunction of Claude and Virgil, noting how one evoked the other. Such evocations are attributable to similarities of sensibility. If, in Claude, we find ourselves in the realm of Saturn, the ruler of the world in a golden age of innocence and plenty, and if, in Virgil, we find ourselves in the same realm, we recognize that there is, as between Claude and Virgil, an identity of sensibility. Yet if one questions the dogma that the origins of poetry are to be found in the sensibility and if one says that a fortunate poem or a fortunate painting is a synthesis of exceptional concentration (that degree of concentration that has a lucidity of its own, in which we see clearly what we want to do and do it instantly and perfectly), we find that the operative force within us does not, in fact, seem to be the sensibility, that is to say, the feelings. It seems to be a constructive faculty, that derives its energy more from the imagination than from the sensibility. I have spoken of questioning, not of denying. The mind retains experience, so that long after the experience, long after the winter clearness of a January morning, long after the limpid vistas of Corot, that faculty within us of which I have spoken makes its own constructions out of that experience. If it merely reconstructed the experience or repeated for us our sensations in the face of it, it would be the memory. What it really does is to use it as material with which it does whatever it wills. This is the typical function of the imagination which always makes use of the familiar to produce the unfamiliar. What these remarks seem to involve is the substitution for the idea of inspiration of the idea of an effort of the mind not dependent on the vicissitudes of the sensibility. It is so completely possible to sit at one's table and without the help of the agitation of the feelings to write plays of incomparable enhancement that that is precisely what Shakespeare did. He was not dependent on the fortuities of inspiration. It is not the least part of his glory that one can say of him, the greater the thinker the greater the poet. It would come nearer the mark to say the greater the mind the greater the poet, because the evil of thinking as poetry is not the same thing as the good of thinking in poetry. The point is that the poet does his job by virtue of an effort of the mind. In doing so, he is in rapport with the painter, who does his job, with respect to the problems of form and color, which confront him incessantly, not by inspiration, but by imagination or by the miraculous kind of reason that the imagination sometimes promotes. In short, these two arts, poetry and painting, have in common a laborious element, which, when it is exercised, is not only a labor but a consummation as well. For proof of this let me set side by side the poetry in the prose of Proust, taken from his vast novel, and the painting, by chance, of Jacques Villon. As to Proust, I quote a paragraph from Professor Saurat:

Another province he has added to literature is the description of those eternal moments in which we are lifted out of the drab world. . . . The madeleine dipped in tea, the steeples of Martinville, some trees on a road, a perfume of wild flowers, a vision of light and shade on trees, a spoon clinking on a plate that is like a railway man's hammer on the wheels of the train from which the trees were seen, a stiff napkin in an hotel, an inequality in two stones in Venice and the disjointment in the yard of the Guermantes' town house. . . .

As to Villon: shortly before I began to write these notes I dropped into the Carré Gallery in New York to see an exhibition of paintings which included about a dozen works by him. I was immediately conscious of the presence of the enchantments of intelligence in all his prismatic material. A woman lying in a hammock was transformed into a complex of planes and tones, radiant, vaporous, exact. A tea-pot and a cup or two took their place in a reality composed wholly of things unreal. These works were *deliciae* of the spirit as distinguished from *delectationes* of the senses and this was so because one found in them the labor of calculation, the appetite for perfection.

3

One of the characteristics of modern art is that it is uncompromising. In this it resembles modern politics, and perhaps it would appear on study, including a study of the rights of man and of women's hats and dresses, that everything modern, or possibly merely new, is, in the nature of things, uncompromising. It is especially uncompromising in respect to precinct. One of the De Goncourts said that nothing in the world hears as many silly things said as a picture in a museum; and in thinking about that remark one has to bear in mind that in the days of the De Goncourts there was no such thing as a museum of modern art. A really modern definition of modern art, instead of making concessions, fixes limits which grow smaller and smaller as time passes and more often than not come to include one man alone, just as if there should be scrawled across the façade of the building in which we now are, the words *Cézanne delineavit*. Another characteristic of modern art is that it is plausible. It has a reason for everything. Even the lack of a reason becomes a reason. Picasso expresses surprise that people should ask what a picture means and says that pictures are not intended to have meanings. This explains everything. Still another characteristic of modern art is that it is bigoted. Every painter who can be defined as a modern painter becomes, by virtue of that definition, a freeman of the world of art and hence the equal of any other modern painter. We recognize that they differ one from another but in any event they are not to be judged except by other modern painters.

We have this inability (not mere unwillingness) to compromise, this same plausibility and bigotry in modern poetry. To exhibit this, let me divide modern poetry into two classes, one that is modern in respect to what it says, the other that is modern in respect to form. The first kind is not interested primarily in form. The second is. The first kind is interested in form but it accepts a banality of form as incidental to its language. Its justification is that in expressing thought or feeling in poetry the purpose of the poet must be to subordinate the mode of expression, that, while the value of the poem as a poem depends on expression, it depends primarily on what is expressed. Whether the poet is modern or ancient, living or dead, is, in the last analysis, a question of what he is talking about, whether of things modern or ancient, living or dead. The counterpart of Villon in poetry, writing as he paints, would concern himself with like things (but not necessarily confining himself to them), creating the same sense of aesthetic certainty, the same sense of exquisite realization and the same sense of being modern and living. One sees a good deal of poetry, thanks, perhaps, to Mallarmé's *Un Coup de Dés*, in which the exploitation of form involves nothing more than the use of small letters for capitals, eccentric line-endings, too little or too much punctuation and similar aberrations. These have nothing to do with being alive. They have nothing to do with the conflict between the poet and that of which his poems are made. They are neither "bonne soupe" nor "beau langage."

What I have said of both classes of modern poetry is inadequate as to both. As to the first, which permits a banality of form, it is even harmful, as suggesting that it possesses less of the artifice of the poet than the second. Each of these two classes is intransigent as to the other. If one is disposed to think well of the class that stands on what it has to say, one has only to think of Gide's remark, "Without the unequaled beauty of his prose, who would continue to interest himself in Bossuet?" The division between the two classes, the division, say, between Valéry and Apollinaire, is the same division into factions that we find everywhere in modern painting. But aesthetic creeds, like other creeds, are the certain evidences of exertions to find the truth. I have tried to say no more than was necessary to evince the relations, in which we are interested, as they exist in the manifestations of today. What, when all is said and done, is the significance of the existence of such relations? Or is it enough to note them? The question is not the same as the question of the significance of art. We do not have to be told of the significance of art. "It is art," said Henry James, "which makes life, makes interest, makes importance . . . and I know of no substitute whatever for the force and beauty of its process." The world about us would be desolate except for the world within us. There is the same interchange between these two worlds that there is between one art and another, migratory passings to and fro, quickenings, Promethean liberations and discoveries.

Yet it may be that just as the senses are no respecters of reality, so the faculties are no respecters of the arts. On the other hand, it may be that we are dealing with something that has no significance, something that is the result of imitation. Quatremère de Quincy distinguished between the poet and the painter as between two imitators, one moral, the other physical. There are imitations within imitations and the relations between poetry and painting may present nothing more. This idea makes it possible, at least, to see more than one side of the subject.

4

All of the relations of which I have spoken are themselves related in the deduction that the vis poetica, the power of poetry, leaves its mark on whatever it touches. The mark of poetry creates the resemblance of poetry as between the most disparate things and unites them all in its recognizable virtue. There is one relation between poetry and painting which does not participate in the common mark of common origin. It is the paramount relation that exists between poetry and people in general and between painting and people in general. I have not overlooked the possibility that, when this evening's subject was suggested, it was intended that the discussion should be limited to the relations between modern poetry and modern painting. This would have involved much tinkling of familiar cymbals. In so far as it would have called for a comparison of this poet and that painter, this school and that school, it would have been fragmentary and beyond my competence. It seems to me that the subject of modern relations is best to be approached as a whole. The paramount relation between poetry and painting today, between modern man and modern art is simply this: that in an age in which disbelief is so profoundly prevalent or, if not disbelief, indifference to questions of belief, poetry and painting, and the arts in general, are, in their measure, a compensation for what has been lost. Men feel that the imagination is the next greatest power to faith: the reigning prince. Consequently their interest in the imagination and its work is to be regarded not as a phase of humanism but as a vital self-assertion in a world in which nothing but the self remains, if that remains. So regarded, the study of the imagination and the study of reality come to appear to be purified, aggrandized, fateful. How much stature, even vatic stature, this conception gives the poet! He need not exercise this dignity in vatic works. How much authenticity, even orphic authenticity, it gives to the painter! He need not display this authenticity in orphic works. It should be enough for him that that to which he has given his life should be so enriched by such an access of value. Poet and painter alike live and work in the midst of a generation that is experiencing essential poverty in spite of fortune. The extension of the mind beyond the range of the mind, the projection of reality beyond reality, the determination to cover the ground, whatever it may be, the determination not to be confined, the recapture of excitement and intensity of interest, the enlargement of the spirit at every time, in every way, these are the unities, the relations, to be summarized as paramount now. It is not material whether these relations exist consciously or unconsciously. One goes back to the coercing influences of time and place. It is possible to be subjected to a lofty purpose and not to know it. But I think that most men of any degree of sophistication, most poets, most painters know it.

When we look back at the period of French classicism in the seventeenth century, we have no difficulty in seeing it as a whole. It is not so easy to see one's own time that way. Pretty much all of the seventeenth century, in France, at least, can be summed up in that one word: classicism. The paintings of Poussin, Claude's contemporary, are the inevitable paintings of the generation of Racine. If it had been a time when dramatists used the detailed scene directions that we expect today, the directions of Racine would have left one wondering whether one was reading the description of a scene or the description of one of Poussin's works. The practice confined them to the briefest generalization. Thus, after the list of persons in *King Lear*, Shakespeare added only two words: "Scene: Britain." Yet even so, the directions of Racine, for all their brevity, suggest Poussin. That a common quality is to be detected in such simple things exhibits the extent of the interpenetration persuasively. The direction for *Britannicus* is "The scene is at Rome, in a chamber of the palace of Nero"; for *Iphigénie en Aulide*, "The scene is at Aulis, before the tent of Agamemnon"; for *Phèdre*, "The scene is at Trézène, a town of the Peloponnesus"; for *Esther*, "The scene is at Susa, in the palais of Assuérus"; and for *Athalie*, "The scene is in the temple of Jerusalem, in a vestibule of the apartment of the grand priest."

Our own time, and by this I mean the last two or three generations, including our own, can be summed up in a way that brings into unity an immense number of details by saying of it that it is a time in which the search for the supreme truth has been a search in reality or through reality or even a search for some supremely acceptable fiction. Juan Gris began some notes on his painting by saying: "The world from which I extract the elements of reality is not visual but imaginative." The history of this attitude in literature and particularly in poetry, in France, has been traced by Marcel Raymond in his *From Baudelaire to Surrealism*. I say particularly in poetry because there are associated with it the names of Baudelaire, Rimbaud, Mallarmé and Valéry. In painting, its history is the history of modern painting. Moreover, I say in France because, in France, the theory of poetry is not abstract as it so often is with us, when we have any theory at all, but is a normal activity of the poet's mind in surroundings where he must engage in such activity or be extirpated. Thus necessity develops an awareness and a sense of fatality which give to poetry values not to be reproduced by indifference and chance. To the man who is seeking the sanction of life in poetry, the namby-pamby is an intolerable dissipation. The theory of poetry, that is to say, the total of the theories of poetry, often seems to become in time a mystical theology or, more simply, a mystique. The reason for this must by now be clear. The reason is the same reason why the pictures in a museum of modern art often seem to become in time a mystical aesthetic, a prodigious search of appearance, as if to find a way of saying and of establishing that all things, whether below or above appearance, are one and that it is only through reality, in which they are reflected or, it may be, joined together, that we can reach them. Under such stress, reality changes from substance to sublety, a sublety in which it was natural for Cézanne to say: "I see planes bestriding each other and sometimes straight lines seem to me to fall" or "Planes in color. . . . The colored area where shimmer the souls of the planes, in the blaze of the kindled prism, the meeting of planes in the sunlight." The conversion of our *Lumpenwelt* went far beyond this. It was from the point of view of another subtlety that Klee could write: "But he is one chosen that today comes near to the secret places where original law fosters all evolution. And what artist would not establish himself there where the organic center of all movement in time and space—which he calls the mind or heart of creation —determines every function." Conceding that this sounds a bit like sacerdotal jargon, that is not too much to allow to those that have helped to create a new reality, a modern reality, since what has been created is nothing less.

This reality is, also, the momentous world of poetry. Its instantaneities are the familiar intelligence of poets, although it has been the intelligence of another ambiance. Simone Weil in *La Pesanteur et La Grâce* has a chapter on what she calls decreation. She says that decreation is making pass from the created to the uncreated, but that

destruction is making pass from the created to nothing-
ness. Modern reality is a reality of decreation, in which
our revelations are not the revelations of belief, but the
precious portents of our own powers. The greatest truth
we could hope to discover, in whatever field we discov-
ered it, is that man's truth is the final resolution of every-
thing. Poets and painters alike today make that assump-
tion and this is what gives them the validity and serious
dignity that become them as among those that seek wis-
dom, seek understanding. I am elevating this a little, be-
cause I am trying to generalize and because it is incredi-
ble that one should speak of the aspirations of the last
two or three generations without a degree of elevation.
Sometimes it seems the other way. Sometimes we hear
it said that in the eighteenth century there were no poets
and that the painters—Chardin, Fragonard, Watteau—
were élégants and nothing more; that in the nineteenth
century the last great poet was the man that looked most
like one and that the whole Pierian sodality had better
have been fed to the dogs. It occasionally seems like that
today. It must seem as it may. In the logic of events, the
only wrong would be to attempt to falsify the logic, to
be disloyal to the truth. It would be tragic not to realize
the extent of man's dependence on the arts. The kind of
world that might result from too exclusive a dependence
on them has been questioned, as if the discipline of the
arts was in no sense a moral discipline. We have not to
discuss that here. It is enough to have brought poetry and

painting into relation as sources of our present concep-
tion of reality, without asserting that they are the sole
sources, and as supports of a kind of life, which it seems
to be worth living, with their support, even if doing so is
only a stage in the endless study of an existence, which is
the heroic subject of all study.

WALLACE STEVENS was born in Reading, Pennsylvania, on October 2, 1879, and died in Hartford, Connecticut, on August 2, 1955. He attended Harvard University for three years, and then studied law at the New York Law School, receiving his degree in 1903. In 1904 he was admitted to the New York Bar and began to practice in New York City. From 1916 to his death he was associated with the Hartford Accident and Indemnity Company, of which he became vice president in 1934.

Although Wallace Stevens had contributed to the *Harvard Advocate* while in college, he did not gain general recognition until four of his poems, appearing in a special 1914 wartime issue of *Poetry*, won a prize. He was awarded another prize for *Three Travelers Watch a Sunrise*, a one-act play later produced at the Provincetown Playhouse, New York. *Harmonium*, his first volume of poems, was published by Alfred A. Knopf in 1923; it was followed by *Ideas of Order* (1936), *The Man with the Blue Guitar* (1937), *Parts of a World* (1942), *Transport to Summer* (1947), *The Auroras of Autumn* (1950), *The Necessary Angel* (1951), *The Collected Poems of Wallace Stevens* (1954), and *Opus Posthumous* (1957).

Wallace Stevens was awarded the Bollingen Prize in Poetry of the Yale University Library for 1949. In 1951 he won the National Book Award in Poetry for *The Auroras of Autumn;* in 1955 he was present to accept it a second time, for *The Collected Poems of Wallace Stevens*, which was also awarded the Pulitzer Prize in Poetry in 1955.